LEARNING LEGAL REASONING

*Briefing, Analysis and Theory**

By Professor John Delaney

Drawings by Anne Burgess

---

*The previous title of this book was: *How to Brief a Case, An Introduction to Jurisprudence.*

Library of Congress Catalog Card No. 83-072289

First Printing	August, 1983
Second Printing	September, 1984
Third Printing	August, 1986
Fourth Printing	July, 1987
Fifth Printing	June, 1988
Sixth Printing	June, 1989
Seventh Printing	December, 1989
Eighth Printing	July, 1990
Ninth Printing	August, 1993
Second Revised Edition	July, 1999

Published by
John Delaney Publications
P.O. Box 404
Bogota, New Jersey 07603-0404
(201) 836-2543

About the Author

Professor John Delaney taught at the New York University School of Law for many years and since 1983 he has taught at the new City University of New York Law School at Queens College. *Learning Legal Reasoning--Briefing, Analysis and Theory* emerged from these many years of teaching both beginning and advanced law students. Professor Delaney has lectured on legal reasoning and law exams at Harvard, New York University and other law schools. Professor Delaney is also the author of law review articles and of *How To Do Your Best On Law School Exams* (1982, 1988), and *Criminal Law, A Problem Solving Approach* (1986), and is the general editor of nine other books, mostly about comparative law, in the *American Series of Foreign Penal Codes*. Prior to teaching, Professor Delaney conducted approximately one thousand trials and he has written and argued more than one hundred and fifty appeals.

For My Beloved Parents

Valentine—Who fought for the freedom of Ireland.

Elizabeth—Who fought for the freedom of her sons.

ACKNOWLEDGMENTS

I wish first to acknowledge the assistance of Professor Lisa H. Blitman of New York Law school. Professor Blitman's valuable ideas, unremitting encouragement and critical evaluations have extended throughout the entire span of the project. Anne Burgess' brilliant and witty drawings adorn this book and the *New Yorker* magazine.

Professor Susan Tucker, Director of the First Year Writing Program at the New York University Law School, contributed ideas and a substantive editing which has materially strengthened the book. Professor Liaquat Naz of the Washburn University Law School in Topeka, Kansas reviewed initial drafts of the book and deepened my understanding. Professor Robert Pugsley of the Southwestern University Law School in Los Angeles, California aided in the substantive review of the book. Professor John Sexton of the New York University Law School clarified issues. Harold Marcus of the New York University, a novelist and a poet, suggested the idea of the book and provided insight.

Johanna De Niet typed the manuscript with her usual impressive competence and encouraged me with her support and grace. Kathy Morahan's valuable copy editing deserves special mention. Lora Eiholzer and Marie Lapidus produced the manuscript with word processing magic and cheerfulness. Betty Tabor single-handedly transformed the first edition into a more eye-pleasing second edition.

I acknowledge too, the assistance of Larry Abramson, Bill Bernstein, Charles E. Blitman, Diane McClain Blitman, Nan Blitman, Nathan H. Blitman, Victor Essien, Jesse Kasowitz, Frank Llewellyn, and Christina Thomas. I also acknowledge that my able students at the New York University Law School have taught me much about legal reasoning over the last fourteen years.

PREFACE TO THE REVISED EDITION

A decent respect for the opinions of others warrants an explanation as to why this book, first published in 1983 and widely used in the first year of law school, is now embodied in a revised edition. Initially, it is worth noting that this revised edition incorporates all the chapters from the original publication. There are no deletions whatever. Rather, two new chapters, VI and VII, are added.

Chapter VI applies the format followed throughout the book to a New Jersey case, *State v. Shack*, 58 N.J. 297, 277 A.2d 369 (1971). Following this format, the *Shack* decision is set forth; an excellent beginner's brief is detailed; certain typical functions of a court which are exemplified in *Shack* are illustrated; and the issues not considered by the court in the *Shack* appeal, as well as the reasons why they are not considered, are also specified. This landmark decision, which appears in real-property casebooks, vividly depicts the application of a policy-oriented mode of judicial formulation, analysis and decision-making. *Shack* also illustrates the impact of ideology, politics and new legislation upon such a policy-oriented approach.

In the final chapter, VII, *"A Jurisprudential Excursus—Modes of Legal Analysis,"* I depart from the format, level of presentation and implicit perspective permeating the original edition. That level and implicit perspective, typical of first-year legal-method materials, is that law is mostly "a technical reality that requires a legal engineering to decode it." The implied message is that if one learns the cases and statutes and the rules for applying them, one can decode the legal mystery inherent in these core legal materials.

In effect, a legal-positivist consciousness is spelled out without explicit acknowledgment. What I now find lacking, therefore, is an explicit introduction to some of the most influential jurisprudential perspectives that underly typical modes of legal formulating, analyzing and deciding. In Chapter VII, I introduce these perspectives by means of a meeting of imaginary appellate judges who critically discuss the cases contained in this book from their distinctive points-of-view. While such jurisprudential discussion may appear other-worldly to some first-year students, I assure you that in law, as elsewhere, there is nothing more practical than a good theory.

May 1987

PREFACE TO THE SECOND REVISED EDITION

The substantive revisions are slight—primarily the changes are cosmetic.

July, 1999

TABLE OF CONTENTS

INTRODUCTION

CHAPTER ONE

CHAPTER TWO

CHAPTER THREE

CHAPTER FIVE

INTRODUCTION

A theme of this book is captured in Blake's poetry:

The cosmos is in a grain of sand.

The cosmos of legal reasoning is in the technique of briefing. It is impossible therefore to learn how to brief without learning about legal reasoning—about learning to read, think, talk and write like a lawyer. Hence, the first chapter in this book is less about the technique of briefing and more about why briefing is important:

- to enable you to understand cases

- to help you understand what happens in class and why

- to introduce you to the basic skills necessary for legal reasoning

- to get you on the right track and to avoid unnecessary confusion

In Chapter I, I therefore present forty answers to commonly asked questions about law and the first year of law school.

In Chapter II, I present a six-step approach to briefing cases. Detailed guidelines are explained for accomplishing each step. Application of the six-step approach with the guidelines is demonstrated with a short, relatively simple, appellate case, *McBoyle v. United States.* Applying the six-step approach with the guidelines, an excellent brief of *McBoyle* is detailed. A contrasting, poor brief of *McBoyle* is then set forth. My comments detail the reasons why the first brief is excellent and why the second brief is poor. Basic functions of a court which are exemplified in *McBoyle* are explained. To aid you in beginning to learn which issues may be reviewed on appeal and which may not be, I succinctly detail a series of issues which were not considered and decided in *McBoyle* and briefly explain why they were not. In a final segment, I define a number of legal terms applied by the court in *McBoyle.*

The basic pattern of Chapter II is then repeated in Chapters III through V. In each chapter, I present a different appellate case (or two) and ask you to apply the six-step approach to briefing with guidelines. Excellent and some poor briefs are set forth. Basic functions of a court illustrated in each case are explained as well as issues not raised and considered. Each chapter concludes with additional definitions of legal terms applied in the case(s) briefed. As you brief these cases, you are also being introduced to legal reasoning, the first priority of the first year of law school.

Too many first-year students misconceive the nature and purpose of law and law school. Many beliefs of beginning students about law school are false or at least misleading. These misconceptions lead to an enormous waste of studying time, blunders in class, exacerbation of beginner's confusion, and a defective preparation for exams. Remember: well started is half done. This short book is designed to get you well started.

The ideal way to benefit from this book is as follows:

First, before starting law school, or as soon as possible, read the book through for an overview. Skip over, however, the examples of excellent and poor briefs in Chapters II through VII.

Second, read Chapter I several times as carefully as you can. Then study the *McBoyle* case set forth in Chapter II and the suggested guideline process for briefing. Brief *McBoyle.* Scrutinize the excellent and poor brief presented and my comments explaining why these briefs are excellent and poor. Compare your brief of *McBoyle* with the excellent and poor briefs set forth in Chapter II. Don't worry about the quality of your initial effort. Study also the sections on FUNCTIONS OF THE COURT EXEMPLIFIED IN *MCBOYLE,* ISSUES NOT CONSIDERED AND DECIDED IN *MCBOYLE,* and ADDITIONAL DEFINITIONS. Study also the illustration and explanation at the end of Chapter II of the various items typically set forth at the beginning of a case (e.g., caption, citation, headnote, etc.).

Third, apply the case briefing process detailed in Chapter II to the *Port Huron* case in Chapter III. Compare your brief of *Port Huron* with the excellent and poor briefs detailed in Chapter III. Don't be discouraged; all beginner's briefs are forgettable. The process of writing awkward, mistake-filled briefs is the path from darkness to light. Study the sections on FUNCTIONS OF THE COURT EXEMPLIFIED IN *PORT HURON,* ISSUES NOT CONSIDERED AND DECIDED IN *PORT HURON,* and ADDITIONAL DEFINITIONS.

Fourth, repeat the process with Chapters IV, V and VI.

Fifth, at this point examine again all your briefs and contrast them with the excellent and poor briefs. Which features of the excellent briefs are reflected in your briefs? Which features of the poor briefs are reflected in your briefs? Correcting and perfecting presupposes diagnosis. Diagnosis requires careful contrasting.

Sixth, in the first weeks and months of law school, your professors will stress many of the points emphasized in this book. Use the explanations in this book (e.g., WHAT IS A PRINCIPLE OF LAW [p. 6], WHAT IS A POLICY [pp. 6-7], WHAT IS THE PRINCIPLE OF A CASE [p.52] to clarify what is unclear. Finally, read the entire book through again after a month or six weeks of classes. Since you'll know much more at that time, you'll see much more in the chapters.

FOR TEACHERS

In teaching first-year students at the New York University Law School, I have emphasized that one of my objectives was to bring students from their beginners' level of confusion about cases and legal reasoning to my advanced, sophisticated level of confusion. I intended the remark as only somewhat facetious. I meant to convey the thought that sophistication in the art and craft of legal reasoning is a life-long task. Almost thirty years of lawyering activity, including a thousand trials, one hundred fifty appeals, extensive law-reform activities, and full-time teaching for many years, has convinced me of the truth of this thought—and of the following principles which underlie this book.

1. Law is a process of reasoning for decision-making about particular controversies. True, it's more than this, but this definition orients beginning students to the overriding priority of first year.

2. The first priority of the first year of law school is the learning of the skills necessary for legal reasoning.

3. It is not knowledge in itself that is imperative but, rather, knowledge filtered through these skills that is imperative for law school and for lawyering.

4. It is important to begin systematically with the basics of legal reasoning, spelling out the positivist form of legal consciousness.

5. It is important to proceed beyond the basics—to introduce a broader jurisprudential framework that explains what judges actually do in case reasoning, beyond positivist formulation, analysis and decision-making.

6. This broader framework requires introducing students early to the flexibility and resourcefulness of lawyerly argument and of judicial decision-making, including modes of reasoning based on the principle of a case and broad and narrow constructions of a case holding and precedent. It also requires an introduction to the frame-shifting possibilities inspired by varying jurisprudential perspectives. Technical craft must be informed by jurisprudential breadth and insight.

7. Legal reasoning in cases is a gestalt; the parts are only intelligible in light of each other and of the whole. Hence, a holistic perspective is a *sine qua non* for comprehending key facts, the procedural history, the issue(s), the holding(s), the judgment, the types of legal reasoning applied, and what each case adds to prior cases already deciphered.

These principles do not emerge from interpretation of my dreams. They emerge from my experience including my debt of gratitude to these giants of twentieth-century jurisprudence, who are my intellectual mentors for the purpose of this book: Karl Llewellyn, Jerome Frank, Edward Levi, Benjamin Cardozo, and Felix Frankfurter. Finally, it may be helpful to understand what I attempt in this book by appreciating what I do not attempt. The book is not about legal research. Nor is it about legal writing in any systematic way. Nor is it about statutory construction in any exhaustive manner. It is about briefing a case and about an introduction to the verdant terrain of legal reasoning and jurisprudence. Any comments and suggestions concerning this book will be appreciated.

CHAPTER
ONE

INTRODUCTION

The questions and answers in this chapter are about the fundamental, not the complexities and exceptions. As a beginner, it is vital that you learn basics before you tackle complexities and exceptions. Otherwise, massive confusion is your destiny. Hence, in these initial questions, I have assumed that you have almost no knowledge of our legal system. I have striven to write concise answers and to resist the temptation to elaborate.

LAW: WHAT IT IS AND IS NOT

What is law?

You may be surprised to know that there is no single definition of law which commands complete agreement. I suggest that, as a beginner, you embrace the following definition:

> *Law is a process of legal reasoning for decision-making about particular controversies.*

Why embrace this definition? Because it is defensible both in principle and in practice. More importantly, it sheds light on what the first year of law school is about. In the first year, the overriding emphasis is on teaching you to read, think, talk and write like a lawyer. To do this, you must develop a set of skills which will enable you to do legal reasoning for decision-making about particular controversies. The suggested definition of *law* matches the overriding emphasis of the first year.

What the first year of law school is not

To understand what you do in the <u>beginning</u> of law school, it may help to know what you will not do.

You will probably not participate in lengthy class explorations of:
> —justice and the requirements of a just society
> —abstract philosophical and ethical questions
> —economic and sociological theories
> —social science research methods, reports and data
> —political issues

Indeed, many of your professors will react negatively to student responses which reflect these "frequencies" of knowledge and analysis because they want to orient you to a legal frequency of knowledge and analysis. Most <u>initially</u> seek to have you read, think, talk and write like a lawyer, not like a philosopher, ethicist, economist, sociologist, researcher or politician.

What are the authoritative sources and types of law?

For your purposes in the first year, the main sources and types of law are:
- statutes
- cases
- state and federal constitutions
- regulations

What is a statute?

A statute is a particular law, or body of laws, enacted by a state or federal legislature in conformity with the procedures required by its constitution, state or federal. Such procedures include the usual requirements of majority vote and approval by the governor or President. Examples of statutes include:

...state penal codes

...the federal penal code

...state commercial codes

...increases or decreases in state or federal taxes

...a state's adoption of "no fault" divorce and car insurance

...the Federal War Powers Act

...appropriations of state or federal funds

...abolition of mandatory retirement for federal or state workers

What is a case?

In a general sense, a case is any judicial or administrative proceeding in which facts of a controversy are presented in technical legal form for decision-making. The object of such a proceeding is to enforce rights and remedy wrongs. A plaintiff is the party (individual or group) who initiates a case. A defendant is the party (individual or group) who responds. Examples of cases:

...seeking money damage for breach of contract

...seeking money damages for injuries in a car accident (tort negligence)

...prosecuting a defendant for robbery (or any other crime)

...seeking a divorce, legal separation, child custody, or child support

...seeking an order from a court directing certain action or forbearance from action by an individual or by any public or private group (an injunction)

In one more specific sense, a case is also the opinion and decision of an appellate court deciding appeals in any of the above-mentioned matters.

A case has two specific functions:
1. it authoritatively decides the particular controversy—e.g., A gets money damages from B for B's breach of contract.
2. it establishes a precedent, or a possible precedent, for the resolution of future controversies with similar facts and issues.

The parties to a case (A and B) are interested in the first function, which determines their rights and duties. As a law student, however, your interest is primarily in the second, precedent-setting function. Much of what you do in class concerns this second function.

What is a constitution?

It is a fundamental political and legal charter for the people of a particular state which is approved by the people (e.g., the Constitution of California) or for the nation (the Federal Constitution). Sometimes called the fundamental law, a constitution defines the character of government by specifying the nature and extent of sovereign power; by distributing this sovereign power (separation of powers); and by prescribing basic principles for the exercise of this power by the three branches of government: the executive, the legislative, and the judiciary. A constitution also typically enumerates the basic rights of the people (a Bill of Rights).

What is a regulation?

Like a case or statute or constitutional provision, a regulation also has the status of law. A regulation is a legal rule authorized by statute (e.g., the Securities Act) and issued by an executive agency.(e.g., the Securities and Exchange Commission) for the governance of matters within the authority of the agency (e.g., stocks, bonds, stock exchanges, selling condominiums in interstate commerce). Regulations are used to enforce the statute and are usually more specific than the statute.

BRIEFING AND THE CASE METHOD

What is the brief of a case?

Very simply, it is an organized, written summary of the important elements of a written opinion. Briefing cases is comparable to diagramming sentences: the parts of a case brief (facts, procedural history, issue, holding, judgment, and reasoning) are analogous to the parts of a sentence (subject, verb, object, modifiers). Briefing, or summarizing, the parts of a case is a way to understand the whole.

Distinguish this meaning of a brief from a second meaning which refers to the formal, written argument submitted to a court at motion, during trial, or on appeal.

What is the case method?

It is a method designed to teach legal reasoning for decision-making (including the substantive law) by analyzing many **appellate opinions** from state and federal appellate courts. It is the dominant pedagogic model used by law schools, particularly in the first year. Be aware that trial courts generally do not write opinions.

THE COMMON LAW SYSTEM

What is the common law system?

It is a distinctive system of law, originated in England hundreds of years ago, in which the king's **judges made the law** throughout the king's realm by deciding numerous cases which came before them. Earlier cases became **precedents** for deciding later cases with similar facts and issues. These cases accumulated over centuries into a vast body of case law. For a long time, the common law was primarily such judge-made case law. In the last century and especially in recent decades, statutory law has mushroomed and is at least as important as case law. The common law system today incorporates a focus on both cases and statutes. In fact, a great number of cases apply and interpret statutes.

The common law is the system of law in England, in the United States, and in the other former English colonies. In the majority of countries, however, the civil law and socialist legal systems prevail. In the civil law system, judges' decisions in cases do not become precedents and cases do not accumulate into case law. The socialist legal system reflects the civil law system and also expresses Marxist conceptions of the state, society and the economy. In all three legal systems, important variations exist from country to country (the United States and England; France and Germany; the former Soviet Union and Poland).

COURT SYSTEM

What is a trial court?

A trial court, state or federal, consists of a judge with or without a jury and performs four basis functions in the administration of legal justice within our governmental system of separation of powers (judiciary, executive and legislature):

1. It determines the facts that are in conflict—**fact-finding**—in particular controversies that are brought before it in technical legal form. It decides which witnesses are credible (believable) and which are not, who said what to whom and who did what to whom, and when. This fact-finding occurs in cases which span the spectrum from criminal law to commercial law, to torts, to copyright, etc.
2. It determines which rules of law from which areas of law are applicable to the particular facts presented—**law-finding**.
3. It applies the rules to the facts—**law-application**—to decide the specific dispute presented to the court. The result is a judgment of the court (a decision of the controversy).
4. It does all of the above applying a prescribed procedure which guides pre-trial, trial and post-trial proceedings (**civil procedure** or **criminal procedure**).

Trial courts are either courts of general jurisdiction, which have power to consider and decide any authorized civil or criminal case brought before it by private lawyers and public prosecutors, or courts of limited jurisdiction, which have power to consider and decide only limited types of cases (e.g., Traffic Court; Family Court; Criminal Court; Probate Court [wills and estates]). In many states, the court of general jurisdiction is called the Superior Court. In New York, however, it is called the Supreme Court. In other sates, it is called the Circuit Court or the District Court.

In our court system, trial courts are either part of the state court system which exists in each state, or part of the national, federal court system. The federal court of general jurisdiction is called the United States District Court. Each state has one or more federal district courts. The federal court of general jurisdiction is called the United States District Court. Each state has one or more federal district courts.

What is an appellate court?

An appellate court, state or federal, hears appeals from the trial courts within its jurisdiction (its purview) in the administration of legal justice. Except in unusual cases, appellate courts accept the facts as determined (found) by the trial court. Appellate courts assess and decide claims that the trial court committed legal error. This is called an appeal. In deciding appeals, appellate courts do not ordinarily consider such factual questions as the credibility of witnesses or what happened on a particular day at a particular time. All of that was resolved by the trial court.

Examples of claims of legal error raised on appeal and decided by appellate courts include: prejudicial rulings by the court in admitting or excluding testimony or other evidence; mistakes in selecting and applying rules; insufficient evidence to prove the case (e.g., negligent tort; intentional tort; breach of contract; arson); and violation of state or federal constitutional provisions.

In many states, the highest court within the state is called the Supreme Court. In New York, however, it is called the Court of Appeals, and in Massachusetts it is called the Supreme Judicial Court. In addition, many states have intermediate appellate courts.

Like the trial courts, the appellate courts are either part of the state court system in each state–or–part of the national, federal court system. In the federal court system, the highest court is the United States Supreme Court. In addition, there is an intermediate appellate court, the United States Court of Appeals, which is organized on a regional basis into eleven circuits.

TWO BASIC COMMON LAW DOCTRINES

What is *res judicata?*

The doctrine of *res judicata* (a "thing which has been adjudicated") means that once a particular claim is finally decided by a court (including appeals) with jurisdiction over the claim and the parties, the court's judgment, and the factual and legal issues underlying it, are considered conclusively decided and may not be relitigated by the parties.

The doctrine of *res judicata* serves the policy interest of barring endless relitigation of claims and the policy interest of judicial economy. *Res judicata* is a doctrine which is strictly applied by the courts.

What is *stare decisis?*

Very simply, the common law doctrine of *stare decisis* ("stand by the decision") means that the decision of a court in one cases provides a precedent (i.e., a standard) for the decision of future cases with like or similar facts and issues in the same or inferior courts within a particular jurisdiction. The rule or principle of law necessary to decide the facts and issues presented in one case provides a precedent for deciding future cases with similar facts and issues. The doctrine of *stare decisis* serves a number of fundamental policy interests in the common law system, including:

> …one meaning of justice: like treatment of like cases
> …a consistent, continuous, and coherent body of case law
> …a reasonable degree of predictability so that lawyers can counsel clients and so that we can all legally arrange our commercial and personal affairs with reasonable confidence about the future
> …authority for judges to build upon past experience, thereby eliminating the need to reconsider old rules of law in each new case
> …fettering the choices and discretion of judges and juries within a framework of the rule of law rather than the rule of whim, arbitrariness, bias or paternalism

While *stare decisis* is a wellspring of our law (in Cardozo's word, "the everyday working rule of our law"), it is not absolute. Exceptions exist and will be illustrated in Chapter V (pp. 79-93).

Binding Precedent

A "binding precedent" means that a decision of a court in a prior case controls the decision in future cases with like or similar facts and issues for both the deciding court and for all inferior courts within the same jurisdiction. Thus, a decision of the Supreme Court of California is a binding precedent for all future cases *[handwritten: Isn't this not true?]* with like or similar facts and issues which are decided by the Supreme Court of California. A binding precedent is both a norm and a prediction. It is a norm because the decision of future cases with similar facts in the same or inferior courts within a particular jurisdiction <u>should</u> be controlled by the precedent. It is also a prediction that such future cases <u>will</u> be controlled by the precedent.

Persuasive Precedent

A "persuasive precedent" means that a decision of a court in a prior case may be accepted or rejected by a court in a new case, even though the facts and issues in the new case are similar. For example, a New York court has discretion to accept or reject the precedent set by the Supreme Court of California in a case with similar facts and issues.

SUBSTANTIVE LAW

What is a rule of law?

A **rule of law** is—An authoritative legal standard—of general application—requiring action or forbearance—used by courts and administrative tribunals—as a norm—in deciding the legal significance—of the particular facts—presented in particular cases.

The two most important sources of rules for the first year of law school are: (1) the laws passed by the state and federal legislatures; and (2) the body of common law (judge-made law) embodied in many thousands of cases in each state. An example of a **statutory rule**, imposed by a legislature, is the requirement that drivers of cars and trucks obtain driving licenses. An example of a **case law rule** imposed by judge-made law, is the requirement that such drivers exercise the degree of case in driving that an ordinary, prudent or reasonable person would use (tort law). An example of **statutory** and **case law** rules operating together is the requirement that such drivers refrain from driving in a criminally negligent manner.

What is a principle of law?

A **principle of law** has the characteristics of a rule (see prior definition); and in addition, a principle:
1. has a more fundamental status in law than a rule
2. has a broader or more inclusive scope or reach than a rule
3. may be used as a basis for creating rules
4. is sometimes used by a judge to select which one of two or more arguably applicable rules should be applied in a particular case

In our system of law, some fundamental principles are explicitly specified in the Constitution of the United States, including:
- the principle of due process
- the principle of equal protection of the law
- the principles of freedom of speech, press and assembly

Other federal constitutional principles are derived from those which are explicitly specified and then embodied into the case law of the U.S. Supreme Court, including:
- the principle that each person has a right of privacy, derived from the first, fourth and other amendments
- the principle that vague criminal statutes are a violation of due process

Many other important principles are <u>not</u> derived from state or federal constitutions but from state and federal statutes an case law, including:
- the principle that private contracts between individuals must not violate public policy (case law)
- the principle that core crimes (e.g., murder, robbery, rape, arson) must have a criminal intent requirement (case law and statute)

It is important to realize that just as rules exist at varying levels of concreteness, principles (and policies) exist at varying levels of breadth. Law spans the spectrum from extreme concreteness (e.g., the rule that an answer to a complaint must be filed within twenty days) to extreme breadth (e.g., the principle of due process).

What is a legal policy?

A **policy** (also known as a **policy purpose** or **policy objective**) is the interest or end expressed or served by a rule or principle.

Examples:

...The prohibition of murder by rules and principles based on statutes and case law, expresses and serves the policy interest (or purpose) of protecting the life of each member of the society.

...The prohibition of rape by rules, also based on statutes and case law, expresses and serves the policy interest (or objective) of protecting bodily integrity.

...The various rules and principles governing the making of a contract (e.g., offer, acceptance and consideration express and serve the policy purposes (or interests) of freedom of contract and promotion of commerce.

...The tort rules spelling out the requirements for establishing negligence express and serve the policy objective (or purpose or interest) of fairness and monetary compensation for injuries due to the carelessness of others.

...The rules of civil procedure, again based on statutes and case law, express and promote the policy purpose, among others, of equal access to the courts.

In addition, a broad policy purpose is sometimes applied directly (like a rule of principle) as a norm to decide individual cases—e.g., the policy norm in a child custody case of promoting the best interests of the child.

Is there consistency in the use of rule, principle and policy?

No. As I stated in my book, *How To Do Your Best On Law School Exams:*

> Do not expect scientific precision and consistency here. What some cases and professors describe as a rule may be called a principle (or doctrine) or policy by others. Principle and policy are sometimes used interchangeably. If you do not expect consistency in these labels, you will not be disappointed and confused. Knowing these labels is far less important than understanding the rules, principles and policies and being able to apply them correctly. A safe approach for you is to follow your professor's usage in each course.

Moreover, many cases are poorly crafted; the quality of the legal writing is obscure, confused and confusing, making it difficult to spot the issue, identify the holding, and make sense of the reasoning. If you find a case confusing, one strong possibility is that you, as a beginner, are confused—and you must struggle to understand. Another possibility, however, is that the confusion is intrinsic to the case. Learning the difference is a skill to be acquired by analyzing and discussing hundreds of cases. Incidentally, the fact that a case is unclear provides no escape: you must, nevertheless, extricate the relevant facts, specify the procedural history, identify the issue and holding, and make as much sense of the reasoning as possible.

SKILLS FOR LEGAL REASONING

What are the basic skills required for legal reasoning?

❑ extricating the key facts
❑ spotting issues
❑ selecting rules and principles
❑ applying rules, especially by interweaving
  of key facts with elements of rules
❑ adroitly using policy
❑ writing in a lawyerly fashion

Legal reasoning is circular. The necessary skills are like a web; they interconnect and overlap. Hence, while skills can be individually identified and analyzed, they must be practiced and learned as a configuration.

What is extricating key facts?

Extricating key facts is a process of selecting from all the mass of facts presented in a written opinion, by a client, or on an exam, those particular facts which have the most legal significance. Facts or a combination of facts which have the most legal significance are those which establish the elements of a legal rule and therefore require or permit application of that rule. **Key facts** are those facts which raise an issue of law. For example, the fact that A and B, business partners, are arguing about how profits should be split presents a business question which has no legal significance; such a fact is therefore not legally relevant, though it may be relevant from a business perspective to an MBA student or relevant psychologically (revealing unconscious childhood conflicts) to A's and B's psychotherapists. But the fact that A then declares, "I've had enough," and shoots and kills B is a fact having legal significance because the rules and principles of criminal law, which proscribe murder, and of tort law, which proscribe assault and battery, attach to the fact that A shot and killed B and make that fact legally relevant, a key fact.

What is issue-spotting?

Issue-spotting is the corollary of extricating key facts. A **legal issue** is simply a question(s) raised by the key facts about their legal significance. To use the above illustration, while no legal issue is raised by A's and B's merely arguing, as a beginning law student questions should spring into your mind about the existence of a legal issue when you read that A said, "I've had enough" and shot and killed B. In criminal law the issue could be identified as follows: Did A's saying, "I've had enough," and shooting and killing B make A liable for intentional murder? Or, in torts, the issue could be specified as follows: Did A's saying "I've had enough," and shooting and killing B, make A liable for the intentional torts of assault and battery?

As these simple examples illustrate, the formulation of an issue in a one-sentence question incorporates the key facts (or some of them) and points to an applicable rule of law. **Issue-spotting** connects the key facts with the rule to be applied.

What is selection of a rule?

Judges in deciding cases, lawyers in arguing cases, and law students in studying for class and exams, select applicable rules to apply to the relevant facts. To illustrate, when A and B argue over the split of profits, it is _not_ necessary to select any rule to resolve an issue posed by such facts. Why? There are no legally relevant facts which raise an issue requiring selection of a rule of law. A and B's business argument does not pose a legal conflict. When A, however, proceeds to shoot and kill B, these are relevant facts which raise a legal issue in criminal law (is A, in shooting and killing B, liable for intentional murder?) and which lead to selection of the applicable rule. The **rule to be selected** in light of these facts is **intentional murder**, which has five elements—(1) intent to kill—(2) manifested in an—(3) act which—(4) causes, factually and legally—(5) the death of another person.

Notice that this rule, as almost all rules, is composed of **elements.** To know a rule is to know its **elements** and to be able to specify them precisely, without surplusage and without omissions.

What is rule-application, especially interweaving of facts with elements of rules?

Interweaving is the blending together of the key facts with the elements of an applicable rule. By so doing, a student and a lawyer demonstrate that the rule selected is applicable because there are sufficient facts to prove each element of the rule. For example, if A insults B, you know from studying tort cases and a tort handbook that the applicable rule is "mere words of insult, even violent insults, are not in themselves actionable." Interweaving the key facts with the rule is illustrated below:

When A, however, says to B, "I've had enough," and shoots and kills B, you interweave these facts with the five elements of the rule of intentional murder, as follows:

> A is liable for intentional murder. When A says to B—"I've had enough" and shoots B—A's intent to kill B is plain. The act of shooting also manifests A's intent to kill and fulfills the requirement of an act. When B then dies from the shooting, the remaining requirements of factual and legal causation and the death of another person are easily met.

Interweaving is the chief skill of rule application.

What is adroit use of policy?

Adroit use of policy in an opinion, on an exam, or in practice stems from an understanding of the nature and function of policy (see p. 6). If you see policies as the ends or interests served by applying rules and principles, you will have a sharper and deeper understanding of legal reasoning and will be better able to decide whether or not a specific rule applies. You will be able to buttress your rule application, especially in close cases, with a succinct reference to the policy served by a particular rule. In novel fact situations, you will be able to apply the policy directly or to argue for application of a new rule to be applied in light of the policy to be served.

Contrary to what some first-year students think, policy is not your latest political hallucination—or mine. Legal policies should not be equated with political policies. Most legal policy is entrenched in the law, embodied in cases and statutes. Many first-year professors stress such policy, not just rules and principles. The best way to learn to identify and use legal policies adroitly is to pinpoint how judges use policies in opinions and to pay close attention to your professors' comments on such usage.

What is lawyerly writing?

Lawyerly writing, the final skill required for legal reasoning, is necessary to apply the first five skills. These five skills—extricating the key facts, issue-spotting, selecting rules, applying rules, and using policy—are neither abstract nor independent of each other. You demonstrate that you possess these skills by displaying them in lawyerly talk in class and lawyerly writing on exams and in legal memoranda.

Lawyerly writing is:
...organized
...purposeful
...direct
...clear
...concise
...complete
...logical (avoiding contradictions, inconsistencies and non-sequiturs)
...persuasive

Lawyerly writing is <u>not:</u>
...rambling
...verbose
...fancy, pretentious or pompous
...conclusory or sweeping
...cryptic or cursory
...abstract or academic
...only about rules, principles and policies
...only factual
...the same as historical, sociological, philosophical, ethical, economic, literary or scientific analysis

THE FIRST YEAR

Why is the first year of law school formidable?

It's like being immersed suddenly in a foreign country and struggling with a strange language. You have to learn a new vocabulary (legal terms), a new grammar (skills in legal reasoning), and conversation (application for decision-making). Some confusion and awkwardness are inevitable.

More concretely:

…Many of the words in cases are purely legal and you must learn their meanings one by one (e.g., *res ipsa locquitur, sua sponte, demurrer, mandamus, certiorari, mens rea, actus reus*).

…Many of the words used in cases which have an ordinary meaning in English also have a technical, legal meaning which is the meaning intended in the cases (e.g., motion, answer, malice, provocation, the reasonable man, intent, trespass, equitable.

…When you begin, you can spot words in the first category, but you won't know immediately which ordinary English words have a special legal meaning (second category).

…Many of the words in the first two categories have multiple legal meanings. While a legal dictionary is helpful, you may have difficulty in the beginning selecting which of the multiple meanings defined in the dictionary is the particular meaning intended in a specific case. Gradually, as you learn these meanings one by one, the mist will transform into clear categories.

…Since law is legal reasoning for decision-making, it isn't enough to understand the above-mentioned, basic skills abstractly. A skill is a habit of performance, not simply an abstract understanding. These skills can only be developed by practice over a substantial period of time.

In developing these basic skills of legal reasoning, am I learning to read, think, talk and write like a lawyer?

Exactly—and this is the first priority in the first year of law school. Indeed, it is fruitful for you to visualize yourself as learning legal reasoning by studying torts, contracts, criminal law, civil procedure, etc. If, over a period of time, you develop and internalize these basic skills—make them part of yourself—you'll use some of these skills each day you work as a lawyer. You'll gradually perfect a lawyerly approach to <u>any</u> legal issue—your reading, thinking, talking and writing will become more precise and vigorous. This is one of the principal objectives of law school. In contrast, contrary to what you believe, much of the subject matter you learn in specific courses (e.g., criminal law, torts) will eventually fade, with the obvious exception of areas of your practice (e.g., wills and estates, real estate, or commercial law).

ROLE OF KNOWLEDGE

You don't emphasize knowledge—I thought law school meant learning the law?

Not in the sense of defining law as essentially a series of rules, principles and policies to be memorized and regurgitated upon proper cue. Not in the sense of seeing a law student and a lawyer as human computers to be programmed (stuffed) with thousands of statutes and cases in thirty or more areas of law.

The knowledge that will help you is the knowledge that empowers you to extricate the key facts, spot issues, select rules, interweave, use policy and write in a lawyerly way. It is <u>not</u> knowledge in itself that will help you but knowledge filtered through these basic skills. Knowledge is not an end in itself but a means to the end of legal reasoning for decision-making. **Knowledge is, then, absolutely necessary and absolutely insufficient.**

The false idea that law and the learning of law are primarily a matter of memorizing and regurgitating is a classic, first-year blunder. Avoid it.

BRIEFING AND SKILLS

How does briefing help me to learn and practice the basic legal skills necessary for legal reasoning?

The appellate cases which you brief in law school illustrate the use of the basic skills necessary for legal reasoning. Specifically, in writing an appellate decision, the judge:
—identifies and marshals the key facts —
—identifies the legal issue raised by the facts —
—selects the applicable rule of law and incorporates the rule into a holding—
—interweaves the elements of that rule with the key facts —
—sometimes uses policy to buttress the reasoning—
—does all of the above with lawyerly writing—

Each case is a vivid demonstration of the basic skills necessary for legal reasoning.

In briefing appellate cases, you identify and analyze each part of the decision which exemplifies the above-listed, basic skills. For example, you identify key facts, spot issues, identify holdings, etc., as they are presented in the case. Therefore, in briefing these cases and working with their component parts, (e.g., facts, issues, holdings), you practice the basic skills necessary for legal reasoning. The cases present a veritable Milky Way of legal reasoning for decision-making. Case briefing is your telescope.

Am I supposed to learn all about legal reasoning from briefing cases?

No. Briefing cases is one core means for deciphering cases. Other methods include the Socratic method in class, class discussion, lectures, writing exercises, moot court, and study groups.

Do these basic skills of legal reasoning apply in doing other legal tasks?

Yes. They apply in—class discussion—law school and bar exams—written and oral argument for motions, trials, and appeals—everyday legal practice including assessing the merit of cases, writing legal memoranda, marshalling facts, etc.

How does briefing cases help me prepare for class?

Although many beginning students don't realize it, the dominant priority in first-year classes is the teaching of legal reasoning by stressing the basic skills. Typically, students are asked questions about the core elements of the case (facts, procedure, issue, holding, judgment and reasoning). Your case brief provides the foundation for your responses. Moreover, if you are not called upon and do not volunteer, your brief also enables you to follow the questions, answers, discussion and lecture.

In addition, teachers ask hypotheticals—questions about the issues raised in a case or in a series of cases. What you have learned from case briefing enables you to respond and to understand the responses of others and your professor' comments.

Moreover, your professors will stress reconciling and synthesizing of a number of cases. What you have learned from briefing these cases enables you to participate in this process.

What is reconciling and synthesizing of cases?

To learn lawyerly reading, thinking, talking and writing by means of the case law method requires concentrating on a chain of related cases, not simply on individual cases, one by one. Each case is a link in a chain of reasoning. It is this linkage that makes each case important in the case law process and that underlies your professor's insistent question—what does this case add (meaning why is this case significant in light of the rest of the relevant cases)? Once you understand the chain of reasoning in a group of cases, you are able to understand each case more deeply and more sharply. John Donne's line, "No man is an island," is paralleled—no case is an island.

The technique for identifying and analyzing the chain of reasoning in a group of related cases is called **reconciling and synthesizing** cases. It is a legal application of the logic of analysis by comparison, which stresses similarities and differences. The doctrine of *stare decisis* (see p. 5) makes the determination of similarities or differences the crucial step in legal reasoning. Your professor's questions will pinpoint similarities and differences in the facts, the issues posed, rules selected, the holdings, and the analyses. Through this relentless questioning and answering, you unravel the meaning of a group of cases and you hone your basic skills, including your knowledge of substantive law. You therefore increase your legal reasoning ability and your confidence.

THE LAW SCHOOL CLASSROOM

What is the Socratic method?

Inspired by Socrates, the great Greek philosopher, the Socratic method is a series of professorial questions and student answers designed to unravel a particular case, especially within a particular chain of cases. The questioning is designed to teach students the substantive law by practicing the basic skills—e.g., what are the facts; what is the issue; what is the holding; what is the court's reasoning? Other questions typically focus on contrasts and similarities with prior cases—e.g., can you reconcile this holding and reasoning with the holding and reasoning in the prior case? In addition to the Socratic method, you will encounter substantial lecturing and discussion and, if you are lucky, a bit of wit.

In addition to briefing cases, what else should I do to prepare for class?

Read the sections in the hornbook recommended by you professor which cover the issues presented in the assigned class. A good hornbook offers an organized, systematic presentation of the issues and relevant rules, principles and policies. It is comparable to a college textbook (e.g., Samuelson on Economics).

If the cases assigned in torts class, for example, cover self-defense issues, read the corresponding section in the recommended hornbook on self-defense. Exercise self-discipline—read only this section. Otherwise, you'll risk drowning in materials.

The important advantage in reading such relevant hornbook sections is that you can acquire an overview of the substantive law from basics to complexities. This overview helps you to understand what occurs in class—the questioning and answering about cases and hypotheticals, and the reconciling and synthesizing of cases.

What is the value of class participation?

The answer is clear if you keep in mind two realities: (1) the first year is primarily designed to teach you legal reasoning—to read, think and write like a lawyer and (2) the dominant priority in first-year classes is to teach you the basic skills of such reasoning.

By participating in class, you are practicing your listening, thinking and talking like lawyer. Making mistakes is the norm; in fact, you can't develop the basic skills without making mistakes. Over time, participation aids you to internalize and hone the skills.

What are the disadvantages of learning by the case method?

First, the casebooks do not typically present the issues, rules, principles and policies in a systematic, basics-to-complexities order. In short, the substantive law is often confusingly presented. The disciplined use of a good hornbook, however, is an effective remedy.

Second, the appellate opinions reprinted in casebooks tend to concentrate on the complexities and the numerous exceptions, giving some students a warped, exception-obsessed view of the law. Again, the disciplined study of good hornbooks which present the basics, as well as the complexities and exceptions, is an effective remedy.

Third, a range of fundamental lawyerly skills are not taught, or mostly not taught, with the case method. These include skills in:

> ...uncovering facts from clients, witnesses, documents and elsewhere
> ...interweaving
> ...client counseling
> ...negotiating and mediating
> ...writing
> ...motion, trial and appellate advocacy
> ...informal advocacy (e.g., with administrative agencies at federal, state and local levels)
> ...working collaboratively with others
> ...reflecting on the underlying values implicit in cases and the personal choices inherent in different forms of lawyering

Fortunately, these skills can often be learned in clinical and simulation courses. In clinical courses, you represent, under supervision, actual clients. In simulation courses, you simulate such representation. In addition, you can acquire these skills by part-time paid and volunteer legal work. It is a mistake, however, to undertake such legal work during the first year of full-time law school unless economic pressures allow no alternative.

STATUTES

What is the role of statutes and when do I learn them?

Even with the emphasis on the case method of teaching law in the first year, there is considerable emphasis on statutes. First, one of the principal functions of appellate courts in deciding cases is application and interpretation of statutes. Hence, many cases deal with specific statutes. Second, there is an emphasis on statutes in some first-year courses such as Contracts (the Uniform Commercial Code) and Criminal Law (the Model Penal Code or a particular state penal code). Third, some first-year professors stress statutes much more than others. Lastly, in second and third years, most students take courses with a strong statutory emphasis (e.g., wills and estates; commercial law; New York or Illinois or California Civil Practice).

THE BAR EXAM

How will briefing help me pass the bar exam?

The best way for you, as a beginner, to prepare for the bar exam is to forget the bar exam. Concentrate on developing your basic skills of legal reasoning which will serve you well in law school, on the bar exam, and in lawyering. To think about the bar exam now is to engage in "crackpot realism." It's like worrying about the twelfth-grade calculus exam as you begin ninth-grade algebra.

WHAT ELSE?

In addition to learning how to brief cases as a means of learning the basic skills, what else must I learn as a beginning law student?

It isn't enough to learn how to brief cases. You must **actually brief** them. Intellectual understanding is only a prelude to actually briefing numerous cases and thus learning to read, think, talk and write like a lawyer.

You must learn the **fundamentals of legal research**—how to use the law library. Remember that brilliant, experienced lawyers, judges and professors constantly use the law library. In addition, learn, as quickly as you can, how to use computerized legal research systems such as *Lexis* and *Westlaw*. They are fun, quick and effective.

You must learn to **prepare for law exams.** They are different from college and graduate school exams and may surprise you. You will not be astonished to learn that I recommend my own 1982 book, *How To Do Your Best On Law School Exams,* which is in many printings and which is available in most law bookstores and in most law libraries, *How To Do Your Best On Law School Exams* and this book complement each other by embodying common themes, attitudes and methods which I believe will be most helpful to you.

CHAPTER

TWO

INTRODUCTION

What you have learned from studying the questions and answers in the first chapter is at best only a prelude—a stage setter. It is not enough to know about briefing cases; you must also be able to do it. If at all times you keep in mind that law is legal reasoning for decision-making about particular controversies, you have the right "head set" for developing the necessary legal skills.

In this chapter, I first explain the steps for briefing an appellate case and detail guidelines for performing each step. Next, I demonstrate the briefing process step by step using a short, simple case. An excellent brief and a poor brief are set forth.

I then explain two particular court functions exemplified in this case. I identify the issues not considered and decided by the court's opinion and explain why these issues were not considered. Lastly, the chapter concludes with additional definitions arising mainly from the briefed case and with explanations of the caption, citation and various other typical items which appear at the beginning of a case.

STEPS FOR BRIEFING

The first requirement for briefing a case is to read it carefully at least two or three times. As you read, concentrate on the six steps for briefing:

- ❏ Facts
- ❏ Procedural History
- ❏ Issue
- ❏ Holding
- ❏ Judgment
- ❏ Reasoning

FACTS (F)—The most relevant legal facts, often called the **key facts**, are those facts which pose a question about their legal significance because they seem to establish the elements of an applicable rule of law.

PROCEDURAL HISTORY (P)—The procedural history of a case identifies which party won at the trial level and which party is appealing now in which appellate court.

how can we "spot" rules of law if we don't know what the rules are?

ISSUE (I)—The issue(s) in controversy is the question presented by the key facts in light of an apparently applicable rule of law. In order to decide the case, the court must answer the legal question presented by the issue.

HOLDING (H)—A holding is the court's direct response to the issue in controversy. It is that rule of law applied to the key facts of the case which is necessary to decide the particular controversy.

JUDGMENT (J)—The judgment is the result or disposition of the case and is usually found at the end of the appellate court's opinion, e.g., "judgment for the plaintiff affirmed" or "judgment for the defendant reversed."

REASONING (R)—The reasoning is the court's explanation and justification for its holding.

Briefing Cases is Like Playing Checkers

Even this initial outline of the six steps for briefing cases demonstrates that the steps overlap and are inextricably interwoven; each step, like each strand in a spider's web, depends on the others. Briefing cases is also like playing checkers or chess. Just as each move in checkers or chess is made in light of both prior moves and future moves and an overall strategy for the game, each step in briefing has meaning both in itself and also as part of a series of steps and an overall approach to the brief.

GUIDELINES FOR PERFORMING EACH STEP

I detail below guidelines for performing each of the six steps for briefing. I have broken down each step into its component parts. At first, the application of these guidelines may seem too detailed and complex. If you struggle in the beginning, however, the application of the guidelines will become easy, almost second nature. In struggling, you will also learn about legal reasoning. Learning to apply these guidelines is like learning to drive a car with a manual, "stick" shift. At first, it is perplexing. With practice, however, it becomes almost second nature. In presenting these guidelines, I first list them in capsule form and then elaborate on each one separately. Where the guidelines overlap, I indicate that fact.

FACTS

SIX GUIDELINES FOR EXTRICATING THE KEY FACTS

- Identify parties and their roles.
- Identify plaintiff's cause-of-action.
- Identify the element(s) of the cause-of-action which poses the conflict.
- Identify the facts most relevant to this element(s).
- Identify defense and its particular element(s) in question.
- Identify the facts most relevant to this element(s).

The parties and their role—Start by identifying the parties to the case and their roles in the case, both at trial and on appeal. For example, the parties may be the plaintiff-seller against the defendant-buyer in contracts; or the plaintiff-wife against the defendant-husband in tort negligence; or the state (or government) against the defendant in criminal law. Simply use the labels applied by the court to describe the parties. Typically, these are appellant-appellee; petitioner-respondent; plaintiff-defendant; state(or government)-defendant. A word of caution: realize that the defendant at trial may become the appellant (or petitioner or plaintiff) on appeal; the plaintiff (or state) at trial may become the appellee (or respondent or defendant) on appeal. Distinguish the trial and appellate levels and any differences in labels.

The plaintiff's cause-of-action—The cause of action is the plaintiff's legal claim against the defendant. Thus, your factual summary should specify the cause-of-action which the plaintiff (or state) alleged at trial against the defendant; e.g., breach of contract, tort negligence, robbery. The court's decision determines the legal rights and duties of the parties arising from that claim.

The element(s) at issue and relevant facts—The factual summary presented in an appellate opinion generally focuses on a particular segment of the facts detailed in the trial court record because many case on appeal concern a conflict over the existence of a particular element(s) necessary to establish the plaintiff's cause-of-action. The facts relating to this element(s) are often called key facts. The search for the key facts also entails a search for the element(s) of the claim which poses the conflict on appeal. Key facts are those which are crucial for establishing, or not establishing, the element(s) at issue.

For example, in a cause-of-action for damages for breach of contract, the only element in dispute may be the element of acceptance, which is one of the elements necessary to form a contract (offer, acceptance, consideration). The facts about this claimed acceptance, or at least some of them, are key facts. If you can zero in on the element in dispute, you are close to finding the key facts.

Any asserted defense, element(s) at issue, and relevant facts—You repeat the process outlined above with regard to any defense _emphasized_ in the appellate court's marshalling of the facts. Again, if you can zero in on the particular element(s) of such defense which is in conflict, you are close to determining the key facts or some of them.

Hints for extricating key facts

You can often tell from how the appellate court organizes its written opinion and from the language it uses, what the court considers to be the key facts. For example, the court may emphasize the key facts by mentioning them first; however, some judges distribute key facts throughout the opinion and others present facts in chronological order throughout the opinion so that the facts mentioned first are simply the earliest occurring facts in a series of events and may or may not be the most relevant.

Pay special attention to the court's explicit characterization of which facts it considers most significant— e.g., "it is important…;" or "what is decisive here…" or "the Court determines…" but be careful that what follows specifies facts, not the holding or reasoning. Look too for sheer repetition of certain facts.

Don't be fooled by an appellate court's summary of allegations of fact by the plaintiff or by the defendant at trial; "the plaintiff contended…" or "the defendant maintained…." Such a summary, however, is often followed in the opinion by the court's specification of the key facts upon which it relies.

PROCEDURAL HISTORY

The purpose of this segment of your brief is to pinpoint the current procedural status of the case. You are already familiar with the first two guidelines.

FIVE GUIDELINES FOR DETERMINING PROCEDURAL HISTORY

- Identify parties and their roles.
- Identify plaintiff's cause-of-action at trial.
- Identify trial court's disposition of cause-of-action.
- Identify which party appealed to which court and the relief requested.
- Identify any prior action taken by an intermediate appellate court.

The parties and their roles at trial and on appeal—This guideline is the same as the comparable guideline suggested for determining the key facts (see p. 16).

The plaintiff's cause-of-action in the trial court—This guideline is the same as the comparable guideline suggested for determining the key facts (see p. 16), except that you need not focus on the elements of the cause-of-action.

The disposition of the plaintiff's cause-of-action in the trial court—The disposition is the result, that is, who won and who lost what in the trial court. For example, there may have been a judgment of conviction of the defendant for robbery in a criminal case, or a judgment dismissing the plaintiff's complaint alleging a cause-of-action for breach of contract.

It's important to identify the exact trial court disposition of the plaintiff's cause-of-action in order to understand the issue in controversy on appeal. Did the trial court, for example, grant the plaintiff or defendant summary judgment in response to a pre-trial motion? Or did the trial court dismiss the plaintiff's cause-of-action during trial because the plaintiff failed to establish a *prima facie* case? Or did the judge and jury find for the plaintiff or defendant at the conclusion of the trial?

Determine who is appealing and for what relief—The party appealing may be called the plaintiff, the petitioner, or the appellant. The responding party may be called the defendant, the respondent or the appellee. Identifying which party is asking for exactly what relief helps you to understand the appellate court's response. Usually the party appealing is the losing party in the trial court and usually such party is asking for a reversal of the trial court's judgment. Look at the beginning of the appellate court's opinion for the court's identification of which party is appealing for what relief.

Any prior action or disposition by an intermediate appellate court—Many of the cases you brief will be direct appeals from a trial court. In other cases, you brief cases which already have been decided by an intermediate appellate court. Thus, the current case may be an appeal from a judgment of the intermediate appellate court which affirmed or reversed a judgment of the trial court. Know the difference between these two types of appellate case.

ISSUE-SPOTTING

The purpose of this segment of your brief is to spot and specify the issue(s) in controversy in the case on appeal. The issue(s) in controversy is that issue(s) which must be decided by the appellate court to resolve the appeal. Keep in mind that there are many possible issues at pre-trial, trial and appellate stages of a case. Since you are studying appellate court opinions, you will concentrate on the issue(s) in controversy on appeal. Other issues in the case, possibly many, have already been resolved at the trial stage. Issue-spotting is a core lawyerly skill. Issue-spotting in appellate opinions is a necessary step in the cultivation of this core skill.

I suggest the following guidelines for issue-spotting in appellate opinions. You will note that these guidelines are similar to the guidelines for extracting the key facts (see pp. 16-17).

FIVE GUIDELINES FOR ISSUE-SPOTTING

- Identify plaintiff's cause-of-action and its elements
- Identify element(s) of cause-of-action which poses the conflict on appeal.
- Identify appellate court's marshalling of the facts.
- Repeat steps above regarding any defense emphasized by Court.
- Formulate the issue(s) in controversy.

The plaintiff's cause-of-action at trial and its elements—To pinpoint the issue in controversy on appeal, you must first identify the cause-of-action asserted by the plaintiff against the defendant in the trial court (e.g., tort negligence, breach of contract, trespass) and the elements necessary to establish that case-of-action. These elements are often mentioned in the court's opinion. If not, you can determine by reading your casebook, a hornbook, a good outline, or from class discussion.

The particular element(s) of that cause-of-action which poses the conflict on appeal and the court's marshalling of facts on this element—Often in appellate opinions the issue in controversy concerns a particular element of the cause-of-action. For example, in the *McBoyle* case later in this chapter, the issue in controversy arises from one such element. So the court's analysis focuses on that element and the facts pertaining to it. At trial, there may have been a number of issues in conflict which are no longer at issue on appeal. On appeal, therefore, there may be only one main question (one issue in controversy), though in some appellate cases there may be two or three or even more issues.

Any defense, its particular element, and marshalling of facts—The issue(s) in controversy on the appeal may also concern a particular element of a defense asserted by the defendant to the plaintiff's cause-of-action. How do you verify whether or not there is such a defense? The court's opinion provides the answer. Does its marshalling of facts from the trial record focus on a defense (e.g., a claim of contributory negligence to the tort negligence, cause-of-action; a claim that no contract existed to the breach of contract, cause-of-action; or a claim of consent to the trespass cause-of-action).

Formulate the issue in controversy—The issue in controversy incorporates the key facts in a one sentence question which refers to the cause-of-action (the legal rule) and pinpoints the element(s), or its particular language, which is the source of the conflict between the parties on appeal. More specifically, this one sentence formulation of the issue(s) in question form contains:

1. the key facts, or some of them
2. the particular element, or language, of either the cause-of-action or the defense about which there is a question on appeal
3. reference to the rule which requires the element.

Correct statements of the issue

An example of a statement of the issue in controversy in a one sentence question is:

> • Did A's being pushed against B in a crowded subway car during rush hour constitute an offensive touching by A as required for the intentional tort of battery?

This example illustrates the three components of an issue, as follows:
key facts: *A was pushed against B in a crowded subway car during rush hour*
particular element of battery: *An offensive touching;* and
reference to the applicable rule: *Intentional tort of battery.*

Another example of a statement of the issue in controversy is:

> • Did A have the requisite intent to burn a structure as required for arson when, while burning leaves in his backyard, a tornado suddenly appeared, spread A's fire to ten nearby houses and destroyed them?

The three parts of this issue could be identified as follows:
key fact: *Sudden tornado spread A's leaf-burning fire in his backyard to ten nearby houses and destroyed them.*
particular element of arson: *Intent to burn a structure.*
reference to the applicable rule: *Arson.*

Incorrect statements of the issue

One way to appreciate correct formulations of an issue is to understand exactly why incorrect formulations are wrong. The following two formulations are incorrect:

- Is the defendant liable for the intentional tort of battery?
- Is A liable for arson?

The common vice in both formulations of the issue is that they fail to incorporate any key facts. Both inquire about liability in the form of pure legal conclusions. All cases, however, determine liability about particular facts. There is no issue and no liability without such facts. This is expressed well by an Iowa court:

> "It is almost a legal maxim that out of the facts the law arises since, if there be no state of facts, there can be no question of law.".

Hence, a formulation of an issue must include at least some of the key facts.

Examples of another type of incorrect formulation of issues follows:

- Was A pushed against B in the crowded subway car during rush hour?
- Was A's leaf-burning fire in his backyard spread by the sudden tornado to ten nearby houses destroying them?

The common defect in these two formulations of the issue is that they are purely factual. They fail to raise a question about the legal significance of these facts. Cases, however, not only inquire about fact. They also inquire about their legal significance. Hence, a formulation of an issue must also raise a question about liability (e.g., for battery; for arson; for breach of contract).

Hints for formulating issues

First, most first-year professors want you to be quite specific in framing issue. One reason is that courts, contrary to what some beginning students believe, ordinarily decide cases on the narrowest ground (issue) presented by the facts. Often the narrowest ground is a procedural issue. Courts do not imitate Zeus in hurling thunderbolts from Mount Olympus. Many of your professors therefore insist on narrow framings of issues.

Second, sometimes courts in opinions specify which issues are presented by the case. This negative formulation can help you to zero in on the issue(s) which is raised.

Third, it makes sense as you meticulously read to search for an explicit statement by the court of the issue presented in the case. Explicitly stated issues are often plainly expressed: "the issue presented is whether..."; or "the question in this case is whether..."; or comparable language. Sometimes the issue is implicit, not explicit; or an explicitly stated issue may be stated imprecisely or even incorrectly. In these situations, you must extricate the issue from the case. Examples follow in this and later chapters.

HOLDING

If the issue in controversy poses the question which must be resolve to decide the appeal, the holding is the court's resolution, the answer to that question. Thus, the guidelines for determining the holding are simple.

TWO GUIDELINES FOR DETERMINING HOLDINGS

- Identify the issue in controversy in the appellate court opinion.
- Identify the holding by extricating the answer to this issue.

The holding is usually one sentence, a declarative sentence which identifies:

1. the key facts, or some of them
2. the particular element, or language, of the rule (either the cause-of-action or the defense) which presents the crux of the dispute on appeal
3. the rule which requires the element.

Correct statement of holdings

An example of a correct statement of a holding is:

- A's being pushed against B in a crowded subway during rush hour was not an offensive touching by A as required for the intentional tort of battery.

The breakdown of this holding into its three constituent parts is identical with the previous breakdown for the related issue into three parts (see p. 19). The only difference between the statement of the issue and the statement of the holding is that the issue is in the form of a question and the holding is in the form of a declarative sentence.

Another example of a correct statement of a holding is:

- A did not have the intent to burn a structure as required for arson when a tornado suddenly appeared and spread A's leaf-burning fire in his backyard to ten nearby houses and destroyed them.

This holding, too, can be broken down into the identical three parts as can the statement of the related issue. Identify these three parts (see p. 19).

Incorrect statements of holdings

Incorrect statements of holdings parallel incorrect statements of issues. For example:

- The defendant is liable for the intentional tort of battery (see p. 20)
- A is not liable for arson (see p. 20)

Again, the vice is that these holdings contain no facts. They are pure legal conclusions (see p. 20)

You should be able to determine the weakness in the following holdings.

- A was pushed against B in the crowded subway car during rush hour.
- A's leaf-burning fire in his backyard was spread to ten nearby houses, destroying them.

Again, the defect here is that these holdings are purely factual (see p. 20).

Hints for determining holdings

Just as you searched the opinion for an explicit statement of the issue, you must also search for an explicit statement of the holding: "the holding is..."; or "we hold..."; or sometimes "we conclude..." or "we find...." Be careful, the latter two statements are often not the holding but rather a conclusion in the reasoning or a factual conclusion.

As in issue-spotting, sometimes the holding is implicit rather than explicit. In these situations, you must extricate the holding from the case. Sometimes, too, the explicit holding by the court is cryptic, imprecise, or even incorrect. Here, again, you must extricate the correct holding. Examples of implicit and incorrect holdings follow in this and later chapters.

JUDGMENT

The **judgment** is the disposition of the appellate case you are briefing. It's also called the **result**. In the language of systems analysis, it's the output of the case. In the vernacular, the judgment announces who won and who lost what. It should always be distinguished from the holding of the case. While the judgment may be mentioned early in an appellate opinion, the judgment is almost always specified at the end of the opinion and is therefore easy to identify.

THREE GUIDELINES FOR DETERMINING JUDGMENTS

- Identify judgment of trial court.
- Identify judgment of intermediate appellate court.
- Identify judgment of appellate case which you are briefing.

The trial court's judgment—who won what in the trial court. You have already accomplished this step in determining the procedural history of the case (see p. 17).

The judgment of the intermediate appellate court—if there was intermediate appellate court review, does this judgment affirm, reverse, or modify the trial court's judgment? Again, you have already accomplished this step in figuring out the procedural history (see p. 17).

The judgment of the current appellate court—almost always located at the end of the opinion—e.g., judgment for plaintiff affirmed; or judgment for defendant reversed.

If there was no intermediate appellate court review, the judgment referred to is the trial court judgment. Remember that in many states there is no intermediate appellate court. Remember, too, that in many instances the opinion you are briefing is an opinion of an intermediate appellate court. If, however, there was an intermediate appellate court opinion, and the current judgment is by the highest appellate court in a state (often called the **supreme court**), then the judgment of such court will affirm, reverse, or modify the judgment of the intermediate appellate court (see Judgment, pp. 38-39).

REASONING

After briefing the facts, procedural history, issue, holding and judgment, you are ready to dissect the reasoning: the court's explanation and justification for its holding, its resolution of the issue in controversy. While courts need not explain and justify their holdings, there is a powerful tradition which usually leads to such explanation and justification by *appellate* courts. A court's decision (its holding and judgment) is supposed to be rationalized by an appeal to precedent, principle or policy rooted in a repertoire of traditionally acceptable types of legal argument, and not an expression of arbitrariness, mere power, or bias. The court's reasoning is an effort to demonstrate that its decision is justified by precedent, principle or policy. This reasoning is scrutinized by judges and lawyers who may apply it in future cases.

THREE GUIDELINES FOR UNDERSTANDING THE REASONING

- Identify the separate arguments.
- Identify the types of argument applied by the court.
- Appreciate the varying weight of different arguments.

Identify the arguments—initially, you must distinguish the reasoning from the holding. Sometimes, this distinction is clear. The court's holding is explicitly stated ("we hold…" or "we decide…") and is not cryptic, imprecise or incorrect; and its reasons are clearly an explanation and justification for its holding.

Sometimes, however, the distinction is not so clear. If, for example, the holding is implicit in the court's reasoning, the holding must be extricated from the reasoning and different judges and opposing lawyers may extricate the holding in somewhat different formulations (see p. 21).

After separating the holding from the reasons for the holding, you must identify the separate reasons or arguments. Hypothesize that there is probably more than one reason embodied in the court's explanation and justification. What is the basis for this hypothesizing? Experience. Most of the appellate cases you'll study will have two or more such reasons.

Be aware, however, that appellate courts do not always specify reasons. The facts may be so compelling, the applicable rule so well established, that there is simply no need to explain and justify the obvious.

Identify the types of argument—learning the law includes learning the repertoire of traditionally acceptable types of legal arguments applied by appellate courts in their reasoning. Where are these types of legal arguments found? A simple but not simplistic, response is that these types of reasons or arguments are entrenched in the case law, in thousands of cases. Your first-year subjects, including contracts, torts, criminal law and property, are history-packed areas of law. The reasons applied by courts are rooted mostly in the vast case law in each area which has emerged over decades and even centuries. Each new case is like a new wave that has been preceded by countless prior waves. It is new but the process is old. Thus, learning each first-year subject includes learning, mostly from the case law, the particular repertoire of traditionally acceptable types of reasoning for that subject—for contracts, torts, criminal law, property, etc. While it is beyond the scope of this book to set forth the particular repertoires for each first-year subject, identifying this task for you may shed light on what is expected.

The general repertoire of traditionally acceptable types of reasoning is vast. It includes the following:

1. arguments based on precedent
2. arguments designed to show a compelling need for the decision in the facts (factual arguments)
3. claims of fairness or justice which require the decision
4. claims of utility or pragmatism for the majority or for a large number of people whose economic, political or social well-being will be enhanced by the decision
5. claims of legal principle(s) which warrants the decision (overlapping with 1, 3, and 4)
6. claims of policy purpose(s) or interest(s) of the law, which justifies the decision, a vast arena of argument which overlaps with 1, 3, 4, and 5
7. claims of logic, including avoidance of non-sequiturs, contradictions and inconsistencies, which crosscut and underpin all of the above arguments and which justify the decision

If you're looking for precise categories, clear definitions and consistent language, disappointment is your destiny. What one judge calls a policy may be described by another as a principle (or doctrine). Arguments explicitly of a factual or logical character often mask hidden policy assumptions. Claims of justice and utilitarian benefit are often confused and contradictory. In contract, the reasoning in some opinions rings with clarity, insight and persuasiveness: it is compelling.

What your professors demand is that you gradually become familiar with this vast repertoire of types of legal reasoning in their concrete exemplification in cases in each subject, and that you manifest skill in class and on exams by justifying your legal position-taking with appropriate use of such arguments. To be comfortable in class and to do well on exams (and in practice), you must sharpen your skill in identifying, categorizing, succinctly presenting and <u>understanding</u> the types of arguments used to justify decisions in each subject. One warning: your professors expect concreteness in identifying and applying such arguments. It's not a matter of mentioning magic general words, say of principle or policy, that counts. Rather, you must identify the <u>particular</u> principle or policy which applies in a case.

Interpreting a statutory rule

While the repertoire of argument is vast, it's not without rhyme or reason. Depending on the type of issue and holding in a particular case, some arguments are available, some are not. First, if you have identified the issue and holding, you may have identified a dispute over the meaning of a statutory rule, or element of such a rule, as the crux of an opinion. The *McBoyle* case set forth later in this chapter is an example of this common type of case. Once you know that interpretation of a statutory rule, or element, is the issue in controversy, you'll learn in this chapter that a particular set of arguments relating mainly to determining the intention of the legislature is applicable. Some of those arguments are detailed later in this chapter by Justice Holmes in the *McBoyle* case.

Applying a judge-made rule

Second, if your briefing of the facts, issue and holding reveals instead that a case-based rule, not a statute, presents the issue in controversy, you'll learn in Chapters III through V that a variety of different kinds of argument is applicable in the reasoning. The exact kinds of argument which are applicable depend on the subject and the specific case rule and facts at stake. For example, the arguments applied in the *Woods* case set forth in Chapter V are quite different from the arguments set forth in *Sauer* and *Greaves* in Chapter IV and from the arguments set forth in *Port Huron* in Chapter III. Nevertheless, all these cases, except *Woods*, present a typical focus found in many cases—the issue in controversy centers on whether or not one or two specific elements in a judge-made rule were established by the facts presented in the case.

For example, the controversy in *Port Huron* centered on whether or not the facts established the element of acceptance necessary for a contract (offer, acceptance, consideration). In *Sauer* and *Greaves,* the standard of reasonable care necessary for a negligent tort (duty, standard of care, breach, factual and legal causation, and actual harm). The factual and policy arguments in the reasoning in *Sauer* and *Greaves* pinpointed this specific dispute. The controversy in these cases did not center on other elements. The specific arguments utilized illustrate how the reasoning in a case can help you to zero in on exactly what is at issue and exactly what is not at issue. See the specific arguments used in the reasoning in a case not as peculiar to that case but as concrete application of **types** of reasoning deeply embedded in our law. Learn to apply these arguments in each subject.

Appreciate the varying weight of arguments—gradually, you can begin to appreciate that not all reasons or arguments in appellate opinions are intended to be of equal importance. Do not assume that if two, four, or six reasons are set forth that the court intends each to be of equal weight. Instead, hypothesize to the contrary and ask yourself—which of these arguments seems to be most important. Look for words indicating weight, including "it is important…" or "what is decisive…." Look too for weight as manifested in the amount of space devoted to each argument.

Let your professor be your guide. Which arguments are stressed by your professor in class? Which are treated as secondary? Which are ignored? If your professor stresses one argument, she or he may intend to teach you about that one argument with that case. The other arguments in the case may not be important at the moment because of your professor's pedagogical strategy. Try to go with the flow of her pedagogic strategy. It will go easier for you in class and on exams.

Dicta

Dicta (*dictum,* singular) means discussion in an opinion which is not necessary to the holding. If you recall that a holding is the answer to the issue in controversy, the issue which must be decided to resolve the controversy presented in the case, you have a criterion for determining whether specific aspects of the opinion are *dicta*. If the discussion seems incidental to the holding, it may well be *dicta*.

Sometimes, *dicta* in an opinion is plainly identifiable. The court may discuss an issue which is not the issue in controversy. Occasionally, such *dicta* may even be acknowledged (e.g., "an issue not presented here is..." or "this appeal does not raise the issue..."). Occasionally, too, judges in an opinion may discuss an opinion which is clearly not on point with the facts and issue in the current appeal. Another example of clear *dicta* is presented in *Port Huron* set for in Chapter III. The court's opinion offered a pedagogic review, among other things, of basic rules of contract law, much of which was unnecessary for the court's decision of the appeal.

Alas, not all examples of *dicta* are plainly identifiable. What one judge believes to have been necessary to a holding, another judge may classify as incidental. What one judge may label as *dicta* another judge may label as part of the underlying principle of the case (see p. 52) or of its *ratio decidendi* (see p. 52). The best way to increase your skill in identifying *dicta* is to observe how judges in opinions classify certain arguments as *dicta* and to listen carefully to your professor's comments on *dicta* in each course.

A Caveat on the Guidelines

Do not expect to be able to apply these guidelines mechanically in every case you brief. The cases are too varied, the facts and issues too diverse, to permit invariable, mechanical application. For example, the issue in controversy in the *Woods* case presented in Chapter V concerns an entire rule, rather than an element or two of a rule. This variety and diversity does not invalidate the guideline approach; rather, it requires modification which is illustrated later.

Application of Guidelines

Let's apply the approach to briefing specified above to a simple, short case decided by the United States Supreme Court. Scan *McBoyle v. United States* quickly in a first reading and then read it meticulously at least two or three times. Then brief the case applying the guidelines set forth above. Do this systematically, beginning with the guidelines for extricating the key facts, and so on. Use the steps suggested previously—Facts, Procedural History, Issue, Holding, Judgment, and Reasoning (see pp. 16-22).

McBOYLE v. UNITED STATES.

CERTIORARI TO THE CIRCUIT COURT OF APPEALS FOR THE TENTH CIRCUIT.

No. 552. Argued February 26, 27, 1931.—Decided March 9, 1931.

* * *

CERTIORARI, 282 U. S. 835, to review a judgment affirming a conviction under the Motor Vehicle Theft Act.

Mr. Harry F. Brown for petitioner

Mr. Claude R. Branch, Special Assistant to the Attorney General, with whom *Solicitor General Thacher, Assistant Attorney General Dodds* a n d *Messrs. Harry S. Ridgely* and *W Marvin Smith* were on the brief, for the United States.

MR. JUSTICE HOLMES delivered the opinion of the Court.

The petitioner was convicted of transporting from Ottawa, Illinois, to Guymon, Oklahoma, an airplane that he knew to have been stolen, and was sentenced to serve three years' imprisonment and to pay a fine of $2,000. The judgment was affirmed by the Circuit Court of Appeals for the Tenth Circuit. 43 F. (2d) 273. A writ of certiorari was granted by this Court on the question whether the National Motor Vehicle Theft Act applies to aircraft.

Act of October 29, I919, c. 89, 41 Stat. 324; U. S. Code, Title 18, §408. That Act provides: "Sec. 2. That when used in this Act: (a) The term 'motor vehicle' shall include an automobile, automobile truck, automobile wagon, motor cycle, or any other self-propelled vehicle not designed for running on rails; . . . Sec. 3. That whoever shall transport or cause to be transported in interstate or foreign commerce a motor vehicle, knowing the same to have been stolen, shall be punished by a fine of not more than $5,000, or by imprisonment of not more than five years, or both."

Section 2 defines the motor vehicles of which the transportation in interstate commerce is punished in § 3. The question is the meaning of the word 'vehicle' in the phrase "any other self-propelled vehicle not designed for running on rails." No doubt etymologically it is possible to use the word to signify a conveyance working on land, water or air, and sometimes legislation extends the use in that direction, e. g., land and air, water being separately provided for, in the Tariff Act, September 22, 1922, c. 356, § 401 (b), 42 Stat. 858, 948. But in every-day speech 'vehicle' calls up the picture of a thing moving on land. Thus in Rev. Stats. § 4,

- 26 -

intended, the Government suggests, rather to enlarge than to restrict the definition, vehicle includes every contrivance capable of being used "as a means of transportation on land." And this is repeated, expressly excluding aircraft, in the Tariff Act, June 17, 1930, c. 997, § 401 (b); 46 Stat. 590, 708. So here, the phrase under discussion calls up the popular picture. For after including automobile truck, automobile wagon and motor cycle, the words "any other self-propelled vehicle not designed for running on rails" still indicate that a vehicle in the popular sense, that is a vehicle running on land, is the theme. It is a vehicle that runs, not something, not commonly called a vehicle, that flies. Airplanes were well known in 1919, when this statute was passed; but it is admitted that they were not mentioned in the reports or in the debates in Congress.

It is impossible to read words that so carefully enumerate the different forms of motor vehicles and have no reference of any kind to aircraft, as including airplanes under a term that usage more and more precisely confines to a different class. The counsel for the petitioner have shown that the phraseology of the statute as to motor vehicles follows that of earlier statutes of Connecticut, Delaware, Ohio, Michigan and Missouri, not to mention the late Regulations of Traffic for the District of Columbia, Title 6. c. 9, § 242, none of which can be supposed to leave the earth.

Although it is not likely that a criminal will carefully consider the text of the law before he murders or steals, it is reasonable that a fair warning should be given to the world in language that the common world will understand, of what the law intends to do if a certain line is passed. To make the warning fair, so far as possible the line should be clear. When a rule of conduct is laid down in words that evoke in the common mind only the picture of vehicles moving on land, the statute should not be extended to aircraft, simply because it may seem to us that a similar policy applies, or upon the speculation that, if the legislature had thought of it, very likely broader words would have been used. *United States v. Thind,* 261 U. S. 204, 209.

Judgment reversed.

The Process of Briefing *McBoyle* by Applying the Guidelines

FACTS

By applying the first guideline—**identification of the parties and their roles** (see p. 16)—you identify that at trial the government was the plaintiff and McBoyle was the defendant.

By applying the second guideline—**identification of plaintiff's cause-of-action and its elements** (see p.16)—you identify a federal crime, Section 3 of the National Motor Vehicle Theft Act, as the government's cause-of-action against McBoyle at trial. You next identify the elements of this cause of action:

    A) whoever
    B) transports (or causes to be transported
    C) in interstate (or foreign) commerce
    D) a motor vehicle * *this element seems to pose the conflict (making it a key fact??)*
    E) knowing it to have been stolen -- **is liable**

By applying the third guideline—**identification of the elements(s) of the cause-of-action which poses the conflict on appeal** (see p. 17)—you identify element D above as the element which seems to pose the conflict on this appeal. You should specify, as the Court did, the definition of **motor vehicle** set forth in Section 2 of the Act: "*...an automobile, an automobile truck, automobile wagon, motor cycle, or any other self-propelled vehicle not designed for running on rails.*"

By applying the fourth guideline—**identification of facts most relevant to the element(s) which poses the conflict on appeal** (see p. 17)—you identify the facts which seem most relevant to this element. In this case, the facts are simple, short and are set forth in conclusory form at the beginning of the opinion:

> McBoyle was convicted of violating the National Motor Vehicle Theft Act by transporting from Illinois to Oklahoma an airplane he knew to have been stolen.

With respect to the fifth and sixth guidelines—**identification of any defense and its element(s) in question on appeal** and **the facts most relevant to this element(s)** (see p. 17)—it is unnecessary to apply these guidelines in briefing *McBoyle*. Why? The Court's opinion does not <u>stress</u> a defense and thus, the application of the first four guidelines is adequate here.

Hence, your statement of the facts might be as follows::

Facts
McBoyle v. U.S.
283 U.S. 25 (1931)

The petit. on appeal, McBoyle, was prosecuted by the fed. govern. and convicted at trial of violating the Nat. Motor Veh. Theft Act for transporting an airplane from Ill. to Okla., knowing plane to have been stolen.

That Act (Sec. 3) specifies that
    A) whoever
    B) transports (or causes to be transported)
    C) in interstate (or foreign) commerce
    D) a motor vehicle
    E) knowing it to have been stolen -- **is liable**

Section 2 of Act defines **motor vehicle** as "automobile, auto truck, auto wagon, motor cycle or any other self-propelled vehicle not designed for running on rails."

PROCEDURAL HISTORY

By extricating the key facts, you have already identified the information sought in these three guidelines—**parties, cause of action**, and **disposition by trial court** (see pp. 17-18).

By applying these guidelines—**identification of appealing party and court, relief requested** and **any disposition by intermediate appellate court** (see p. 17)—you identify that McBoyle is the petitioner in the United States Supreme Court. He has been granted a *writ of certiorari* to appeal to the Supreme Court. He seeks reversal of the affirmance by the U.S. Court of Appeals (10th Cir.) of the trial court's judgment of conviction for violating Section 3 of the National Motor Vehicle Theft Act. The U.S. Court of Appeals is the federal, intermediate appellate court (see p. 4).

Hence, your abbreviated statement of the procedural history might read:

> Procedural History
> Judg. of convict. of McBoyle by trial ct. of Sec. 3 of Act affirmed by U.S. Ct. of Appeals (10th Cir.)
> & U.S. Sup. Ct. granted writ of certiorari.

ISSUE

You have already identified the information sought in these three guidelines—**identification of cause-of-action at trial and its elements(s); the element(s) of the cause-of-action which poses the conflict on appeal;** and **the appellate court's marshalling of the facts** (see pp. 18-20).

It is unnecessary to apply the fourth guideline—which is repeating the three aforementioned guidelines applied to any defense emphasized by the court (see p. 18).

Applying this guideline—**a one-sentence formulation of the issue(s) in controversy** (see p. 19)—there are two explicit issue statements suggested in Justice Holmes' Supreme Court opinion:

> Issue
> The issue is whether the National Motor Vehicle Theft Act applies to aircraft?

> - or -

> Issue
> The issue is whether the meaning of the word "vehicle" specified in part of Section 2 of the National Motor Vehicle Act—"any other self-propelled vehicle not designed for running on rails"—applies to aircraft?

The second formulation of the issue is superior. Why? It precisely identifies the issue in controversy to be decided by the appellate court. Remember that most first-year professors want you to be specific in framing issues (see pp. 19-20). Understand how this second formulation of the issue in controversy fulfills the three parts of a good statement of issue:

key fact—*aircraft*
particular element or language—*Part of Section 2 of Act: "…any other self-propelled vehicle not designed for running on rails."*
reference to the rule—*National Motor Vehicle Theft Act*

Notice how, in this second formulation, the issue is not focused generally on the definition of a motor vehicle set forth in Section 2 of the Act. Instead, it pinpoints the precise language within that section which raises the issue in controversy. This is the reason why the second formulation of the issue is superior. The first fails to pinpoint the precise language at stake and therefore fails to distinguish between this language and other language in Section 2 which does **not** raise the issue in controversy. For example, an aircraft is plainly **not** a "motor cycle" and **not** an "automobile truck." No issue is raised by this latter language.

Making these distinctions requires that you understand that one purpose in briefing appellate cases is to pinpoint the exact issue in controversy in order to pinpoint the exact holding. Making these distinctions requires meticulous, lawyerly reading of the opinion. You must read like a lawyer in order to think, talk and write like a lawyer.

Overbroad Statements of Issues

With this insight, the defect in the following formulation of the issue should be apparent:

> the issue is whether in federal law the word "vehicle" applies to aircraft.

This formulation is manifestly wrong on its face because it is far too broad: the case deals only with certain words in Section 2 of the National Motor Vehicle Theft Act, not with federal law in a sweeping sense. This mistake overlooks what is central. Courts in deciding cases resolve only the issue in controversy: the question which is posed by the facts considered in light of an applicable rule, an element of that rule and, as here, certain language of that element set forth Section 2 of the Act. Nothing else is decided. What is illustrated here is that our courts proceed case by case, step by step, with intense concern for the limited facts presented in a case.

The vice in the following formulation of the issue may also be apparent to you:

> the issue is whether it is unconstitutional to apply the work "vehicle" in
> Section 2 of the National Motor Vehicle Theft Act to aircraft?

The vice here results from failure to read like a lawyer (meticulously) and reflects a beginner's blunder of inserting into a case what is not here: a constitutional issue.

HOLDING

By applying these two guidelines—**identifying the question in issue** and **the answer to that question** (see pp. 20-21)—you extract the answer given by the appellate court. Once you have pinpointed the issue in controversy, identifying the holding should be easy. You change the issue in controversy embodied in a question into a declarative sentence. Here for example:

> Holding
> The holding is that the meaning of the word "vehicle" specified in part of Section 2 of the Nat. Motor Veh. Theft Act—"any other self-propelled vehicle not designed for running on rails"—does not apply to aircraft.

Notice that, like the statement of the issue, this statement of the holding is divisible into three constituent parts: **key facts—particular element or language—and reference to the rule** (see p. 21). Notice, too, as in many appellate cases, the opinion in *McBoyle* does not explicitly state the holding. There are no magic words here denoting the holding (e.g., "we hold" or "we decide"). Nevertheless, because you have identified the precise issue in controversy, you can extract the holding.

Overbroad Statements of Holdings

You should be able to appreciate that the following statement of the holding is less precise because it fails to specify what words in Section 2 of the Act make Section 3 of the Act inapplicable to aircraft.

> the holding is that Section 2 of the National Motor Vehicle Theft Act
> does not apply to aircraft.

What are the vices in the following statements of the holding?

> the holding is that it is unconstitutional to apply the word "vehicle" to aircraft.

> the holding is that in federal law the word "vehicle" does not apply to aircraft.

The first holding is plainly erroneous. The second holding is a virtual model of overbreadth, of what a holding is <u>not</u>. In legal reasoning, it is a classic beginner's blunder. The case does not deal with the global abstraction of "federal law." Not at all. It deals, as noted, only with certain words in Section 2 of the National Motor Vehicle Theft Act. Beware of articulating holdings in the form of sweeping generalizations. They are wrong. They violate a cardinal premise of legal reasoning: holdings are usually fact-bound, fact-limited, intended to apply only to a limited range of fact situations.

JUDGMENT

You have already identified the information sought by the first two guidelines—**judgment of the trial court** and **judgment of any intermediate appellate court** (see p. 22)—in determining the procedural history of *McBoyle* (see p. 29). You know that there was a judgment of conviction of McBoyle at trial for violation of Section 3 of the National Motor Vehicle Theft Act. You know too that the intermediate federal appellate court, the United States Court of Appeals (10th Circuit), affirmed this trial court judgment of conviction.

By applying the third guideline—**identification of judgment of appellate opinion which you are briefing** (see p. 22)—you identify the judgment of the current appellate court, the United States Supreme Court, at the end of the opinion: *Judgment reversed.* These words, however, are too cryptic for your purposes. You must specify their meaning. For example:

Judgment
The judgment of the United States Court of Appeals (10th Cir.), affirming the trial court judgment of conviction of McBoyle, is reversed. (The effect of this reversal is to overturn the trial court judgment of conviction.)

REASONING

By applying the **guideline—identify the separate legal arguments** (see pp. 22-23)—you first distinguish the holding from the reasons, then you identify and number the reasons or arguments. Since you know the holding, distinguishing it from the reasons is possible. Your identification and numbering of the reasons might look like the following:

Reasoning
A) In everyday, popular usage, the meaning of vehicle and airplane is different. A vehicle runs on land; an airplane flies.
B) State statutes (e.g., Conn., Ohio & Mich.), and weight of federal statutes (e.g., Tariff Act of 1930), agrees with popular usage.
C) No evidence of congressional intent to include aircraft when this statute was passed in 1919—no mention in committee reports or in congressional debate (though airplanes were well known in 1919).
D) Holding serves objective that criminal statutes give fair warning of penalty if "a certain line is passed." Fairness requires a "clear" line.
E) Holding serves objective of judicial restraint. Court will not extend the statute because the policy served is identical in punishing the transportation of either a stolen vehicle or a stolen

aircraft in interstate commerce; or because Congress may simply have forgotten planes and would "very likely" have used "broader words" if it had thought of the matter.

Don't be discouraged if you missed some of these arguments or did not distinguish among them. Separating arguments is difficult in the beginning. It presupposes knowledge that you do not yet have. Gradually, as you practice and know more, you'll see the separate arguments.

Applying the **second guideline—identify the types of argument applied by the court** (see p. 23)—is extremely difficult in the beginning because you do not have knowledge of these specific types of argument in each subject. Nevertheless, you must begin to practice.

From the explanation of this guideline (see p. 23), you should be aware that *McBoyle*, as many cases, raised an issue about interpretation of a statute, or, more precisely, posed an issue about interpretation of particular language in an element of a statutory rule. A court's power with such issues is limited to determining the intention of the legislature, here the Congress, which enacted the statute. To determine legislative intent, particular types of reasoning or argument are appropriate. Where do these types of reasoning or argument come from? They come from the case law, from the thousands of cases decided over centuries of the common law. Justice Holmes, speaking for the court in *McBoyle*, used a <u>few</u> arguments typical of these types of reasoning. Indeed, the first three arguments in the opinion were all designed to discern congressional intent. They were means to this end.

<u>Discerning Congressional Intent in *McBoyle*</u>

Holmes' first argument was that one way to determine what Congress intended in using the word "vehicle" in Section 2 of the Act was to examine the every day, popular meaning of the word "vehicle." Holmes concluded quickly that in this every day meaning a vehicle runs on land but not in the air.

Holmes' second argument was that another way to discern congressional intent is to examine other legislative use of the word "vehicle," both by Congress and by state legislatures. Holmes concluded that most of this use supports the Court's view. Incidentally, combining the first two arguments is fine, as long as you recognize the two parts of the argument.

Holmes' third argument was that congressional debate and committee reports when the statute was enacted in 1919 revealed congressional intent in this use of the word "vehicle." More exactly, Holmes' point here was that the absence of any mention of airplanes in such debate and reports in 1919, when airplanes were well known, supported the Court's view that Congress did not intend airplanes to be included in the definition of "vehicle."

Notice how these three arguments designed to discern congressional intent were adroitly presented by Justice Holmes with each argument flowing into and supporting the other.

<u>Policy Arguments in *McBoyle*</u>

In addition to the above three examples of specific types of reasoning or argument designed to determine legislative intent, the Court, speaking through Holmes, applied two policy arguments which are often applied when the issue presented is interpretation of a criminal statute.

The first policy argument applied was that fairness requires that criminal statutes give a clear and fair warning of what conduct is prohibited and of the penalty for violation. Holmes concluded that Section 2 of the Act gave no clear and fair warning that aircraft was covered.

The second policy argument applied was that courts, in interpreting criminal statutes, will not extend their meaning either to rectify legislative omissions or because the extension is desirable. The Congress should correct its own mistakes and omissions.

By applying the **third guideline—appreciating the varying weight of different arguments** (see p. 24)—it is difficult to determine which of the five arguments is more important. There are no explicit words signifying weight such as, "it is important…" or "what is decisive…." More space is given to the first three arguments, but that does not seem decisive here. The conclusion is that the court clearly relied upon the two categories of arguments (relating to legislative intent and to specific policies) and it is not clear that the court weighted one over the other. Nevertheless, differences in weight given to these arguments by your professor might well vary from the Court's apparent weighting.

AN EXCELLENT BEGINNER'S BRIEF

Voilá, an excellent brief of *McBoyle* is a sum of the parts:

McBoyle v. U.S.
283 U.S. 25 (1931)

FACTS

> The petit. on appeal, McBoyle, was prosecuted by the Fed. Govern. and convicted at trial of violating the Nat. Motor Veh. Theft Act for transporting an airplane from Ill. to Okla., knowing plane to have been stolen.
>
> That Act (Sec. 3) specifies that
> > A) whoever
> > B) transports (or causes to be transported)
> > C) in interstate (or foreign) commerce
> > D) a motor vehicle
> > E) knowing it to have been stolen -- **is liable**
>
> Section 2 of Act defines motor vehicle as "automobile, auto truck, auto wagon, motor cycle or any other self-propelled vehicle not designed for running on rails."

PROCEDURAL HISTORY

> Judg. of convic. of McBoyle by trial ct. of Sec. 3 of Act affirmed by U.S. Ct. of Appeals (10th Cir.) and U.S. Sup. Ct. granted writ of certiorari.

ISSUE

> Whether the meaning of the word "vehicle" specified in part of Sec. 2 of the National Motor Vehicle Theft Act—"any other self-propelled vehicle not designed for running on rails"—applies to aircraft?

HOLDING

> The meaning of the word "vehicle" specified in part of Sec. 2 of the Nat. Motor Veh. Theft Act— "any other self-propelled vehicle not designed for running on rails"—does not apply to aircraft.

JUDGMENT

> The judgment of the United States Court of Appeals (10th Cir.), affirming the trial court judgment of conviction of McBoyle, is reversed. (The effect of this reversal is to overturn the trial court judgment of conviction).

REASONING

Determining Congressional Intent

1) In everyday, popular usage, the meaning of vehicle and airplane is different. A vehicle runs on land; an airplane flies.

2) State statutes (e.g., Conn., Ohio and Michigan), and weight of federal statutes (e.g., Traffic Act of 1930) agree with popular usage.

3) No evidence of congressional intent to include aircraft when this statute was passed in 1919—no mention in committee reports or in congressional debate (though airplanes were well known in 1919).

POLICY

4) Holding serves objective that criminal statutes give fair warning of penalty if "a certain line is passed." Fairness requires a "clear" line.

5) Holding serves objective of judicial restraint. Court will not extend the statute because policy served is identical in punishing the transporting of either a stolen vehicle or a stolen aircraft in interstate commerce; or because Congress may simply have forgotten planes and would "very likely" have used "broader words" if it had thought of the matter.

A POOR BRIEF

Contrast the above excellent brief of *McBoyle* with a poor brief. My comments on the left specify weaknesses or refer you to a prior specification of weaknesses.

McBoyle v. U.S.
283 U.S. 25 (1931)

FACTS

McBoyle was the defendant in trial court. Here, on appeal, he's described in the opinion as a petitioner. Use label of appellate court to avoid confusion.

The defendant, McBoyle, was convicted of violating the Nat. Mot. Veh. Theft Act. He transported an airplane from Ill to Okla. , knowing it was stolen.

Omission of statement of statutory rule violated (Sec.3) and its elements and definition of "vehicle" (Sec.2). This omission impedes pinpointing exactly what issue is in controversy on appeal.

PROCEDURAL HISTORY

Omits appeal to, and affirmance of judgment of conviction by, intermediate appellate court (U.S. Ct. of Appeals, 10th Cir.).

McBoyle was convicted by trial court and now appeals to U.S. Sup. Ct.

Wrong. Far too broad—see pp.19-20. Where does "aviation law" come from?

Wrong. Again, far too broad—see pp.20-21. Unsurprisingly, a wrong formulation of the issue leads to a wrong formulation of the holding.

JUDGMENT *omitted altogether*

This merely repeats what is in opinion, virtually word for word. The objective, however, is not repetition, but succinct ordering, categorizing and hence, <u>understanding</u>.

ISSUE

The issue is whether in federal aviation law the word "vehicle" applies to aircraft?

HOLDING

The holding is that in federal aviation the word "vehicle" does <u>not</u> apply to aircraft.

(JUDGMENT)

REASONING

No doubt etymologically it is possible to use the word to signify a conveyance working on land, water or air, and sometimes legislation extends the use in that direction, e.g., land and air, water being separately provided for, in the Tariff Act, September 22, 1922. But in everyday speech "vehicle" calls up the picture of a thing moving on land. Thus, in Rev. Stats.§4, intended, the government suggests, rather to enlarge than to restrict the definition, vehicle includes every contrivance capable of being used "as a means of transportation on land." And this is repeated, expressly excluding aircraft, in the Tariff Act, June 17, 1930. So here, the phrase under discussion calls up the popular picture. For after including automobile truck, automobile wagon and motor cycle, the words "any other self-propelled vehicle not designed for running on rails" still indicate that a vehicle in the popular sense, that is a vehicle running on land, is the theme. It is a vehicle that runs, not something, not commonly called a vehicle, that flies. Airplanes were well known in 1919, when this statute was passed; but it is admitted that they were not mentioned in the reports or in the debates in Congress. It is impossible to read words that so carefully enumerate the different forms of motor vehicles and have no reference of any kind to aircraft, as including airplanes under a term that usage more and more precisely confines to a different class. The counsel for the petitioner have shown that the phraseology of the statute as to motor vehicles follows that of earlier statutes of Connecticut, Delaware, Ohio, Michigan and Missouri, not to mention the late Regulations of Traffic for the District of Columbia, Title 6, c.9, §242, none of which can be supposed to leave the earth.Although it is not likely that a criminal will carefully consider the text of the law before he murders or steals, it is reasonable that a fair warning should be given to the world in language that the common world will understand, of what the law intends to do if a certain line is passed. To make the warning fair, so far as possible, the line should be clear. When a rule of conduct is laid down in words that evoke in the common mind only the picture of vehicles moving on land, the statute should not be extended to aircraft, simply because it may seem to us that a similar policy applies, or upon the speculation that, if the legislature had thought of it, very likely broader words would have been used. *United States v. Thind*, 261 U.S. 204, 209.

While Justice Holmes was a distinguished jurist in both the nineteenth and twentieth centuries, his reputation does not rest on his opinion for the Supreme Court in *McBoyle* . The point is not that *McBoyle* was wrongly decided or that Holmes could have used other equally valid arguments from the repertoire of acceptable reasons to justify the opposite conclusion. While commentators speculate as to the Court's motivation in deciding *McBoyle* as it did, its motivation remains elusive. *McBoyle* illustrates what beginners do not know. A substantial segment of trial and appellate cases could be decided either way. In this segment of cases, a court's decision represents its best judgment on the facts and the applicable law. Another court might decide differently. The law is a human institution and hence the level of certainty in the law reflects inescapable human differences. Incidentally, it is illogical, and hence unlawyerly, to conclude, from the fact of uncertainty in decision-making in one segment of cases, that all decision-making is uncertain.

Functions of the Court Exemplified in *McBoyle*

Interpreting Federal Statutes

Courts perform many functions in our legal system. A function performed by the United States Supreme Court in *McBoyle* is its role as the final judicial interpreter of federal statutes. Naturally, the trial judge also interprets applicable federal rules, both statutes and cases, necessary to decide a case. In addition, the intermediate appellate court, the United States Court of Appeals, interprets federal rules as required to decide appeals from judgments of federal trial courts within its jurisdiction. The final arbiter, however, in deciding the interpretation of federal statutes is the United States Supreme Court. Here the United States Supreme Court is performing a function also carried out by the highest appellate court in each state, which is ordinarily the final arbiter of the meaning of its state statutes.

This above-explained function of the United States Supreme Court can also be expressed differently. In *McBoyle*, the Court's power, without a constitutional issue, is to discern the meaning of this congressional statute. The Court has <u>no power</u> to invalidate this statute because no constitutional issue is raised. The Federal Constitution authorizes Congress to enact statutes. In our governmental system of separation of powers, the power of the judiciary is to interpret the meaning of those statutes as applied in individual cases. Congress does not have judicial power to apply its statutes in individual cases. Hence, the issue for the Court is determining congressional intent in enacting Section 2 of this statute, <u>not</u> what the Court thinks the meaning should be.

Principled Decision-Making

In addition, the Court in *McBoyle* illustrates in its articulation of reasons a basic presupposition underlying all decision-making by courts at motion, trial and on appeal in our governmental system. Judicial decision-making is principled, meaning that it is rooted in legal reason and authority, and is not simply an exercise of personal power or power of office, whether mean-spirited or well-intended. This presupposition gives concrete meaning to that primordial principle animating our legal system: ours is a rule of law, not persons. The existence of incompetent, lazy, biased or corrupt judges in no way denies the validity of that principle, which, incidentally, is also well served by many competent, conscientious, fair and honest judges.

Issues not Considered and Decided in *McBoyle* in the United States Supreme Court

One way to understand the particularity and discipline of legal reasoning in the case method is to identify the issues <u>not</u> considered and decided in *McBoyle*, and to understand why these issues were not considered and decided there. These include the following.

Issue	Why Not Considered
The issue is whether or not McBoyle knew the airplane was stolen.	*Wrong. Resolved by the trial court.*
The issue is whether or not McBoyle stole the aircraft.	*Wrong. McBoyle is not charged with stealing the aircraft.*
The issue is whether or not McBoyle transported an aircraft across state lines.	*Wrong. Not the charge*
The issue is whether or not McBoyle transported, or caused to be transported, a motor vehicle in interstate commerce knowing it to be stolen.	*Wrong. That was the correct issue at trial but not on appeal. Appellate courts review certain specific claims of legal error committed by trial courts. They do not simply rehash trial issued.*
The issue is whether or not McBoyle was justly convicted.	*Wrong. Claims of legal error to be reviewed by appellate courts are usually specific and not masked in vague references to justice.*
The issue is whether or not the government's witnesses were credible.	*Wrong. Resolved by the trial court.*
The issue is whether or not McBoyle caused the plane to be transported in interstate commerce (i.e., across state lines) thereby giving the federal courts jurisdiction over the violation and over McBoyle.	*Wrong. Resolved by the trial court and by the United States Court of Appeals for the 10th Circuit.*
The issue is whether or not the federal prosecutor proved McBoyle's legal guilt beyond a reasonable doubt.	*Wrong. Resolved by the trial court.*

The issue is whether or not McBoyle had a good motive or a bad motive for the violation.	*Wrong. Motive is not a legal issue in determining McBoyle's liability.*
The issue is whether or not the trial court conducted a careful investigation of all relevant factual and legal issues.	*Wrong. Not the function of a common-law judge to conduct investigation.*
The issue is whether or not a state court interpreting state law is bound by the U.S.Supreme Court's interpretation in *McBoyle*.	*Wrong. Not the function of the U.S. Supreme Court to decide interpretation of state law. State courts decide such interpretation.*

A FEW MORE DEFINITIONS

Justice Holmes' opinion in *McBoyle* uses some legal terms, and presupposes others, which you should learn and which have not yet been defined. These include the following:

Petitioner—a person who initiates a petition which is a formal, written application to a court requesting judicial action on a specific matter. Here, McBoyle, acting through his lawyer, petitioned the Supreme Court to review the affirmance by the United States Court of Appeals (Tenth Circuit) of his judgment of conviction by the trial court.

Writ of Certiorari—broadly, an order from a higher court (e.g., the United States Supreme Court) to an inferior court to produce the record of a trial for review by the higher court. Typically, it is a device used by the United States Supreme Court to decide which cases seeking review, as a matter of discretion, should be granted that review.

Judgment—broadly, a final determination by a court of the issues presented to it in a proceeding. In *McBoyle*, Justice Holmes states:

> The judgment was affirmed by the Circuit Court of Appeals for the Tenth Circuit.

> This reference to judgment refers to the **judgment of conviction** by the trial court, meaning that McBoyle was determined by the trial court (judge and jury) to be liable for violation of Section 3 of the National Motor Vehicle Theft Act.

In addition, judgment is used again twice in *McBoyle*:

> Certiorari...to review a judgment affirming a conviction under the Motor Vehicle Theft Act.

> This reference to judgment means the judgment of the United States Court of Appeals for the Tenth Circuit which affirmed the judgment of conviction of the federal trial court.

The last reference is at the end of the court's opinion:

> Judgment reversed

> This means that the judgment of the United States Court of Appeals for the Tenth Circuit was overturned by the United States Supreme Court.

Beware of the one-word–one-meaning fallacy. Like many legal words, judgment has different applications. Be exact.

Decision—has many meanings. First, decision is the judgment of a court, at motion, trial or on appeal. "Decision" and "judgment" are sometimes used interchangeably by courts. Second, decision sometimes means the opinion of a court or its holding. Third, decision sometimes means a ruling or finding by a judge on a particular factual or legal issue during trial. Fourth, decision may mean a determination by a government agency or an administrative judge (e.g., after a Social Security hearing). As always, the specific context provides the particular meaning intended.

Intermediate Appellate Court—an appellate court (see p. 4) which considers and decides appeals from specified trial courts, but which is not the highest appellate court in a state or in the federal system. The United States Court of Appeals, organized into eleven circuits, is the intermediate appellate court in the federal court system. The United States Supreme Court is, of course, the highest appellate court in the federal court system. In the states, the names of the intermediate and highest appellate courts vary. In New York, for example, the highest appellate court is the New York State Court of Appeals; the intermediate appellate court is the Appellate Division; and the trial court of general jurisdiction is the New York State Supreme Court. In many states, however, the highest appellate court is called the Supreme Court (e.g., the Supreme Court of California, the Supreme Court of Arkansas, the Supreme Court of Michigan) and the intermediate appellate court is often called the Court of Appeal(s). In addition, many states don't have an intermediate appellate court. Don't worry about learning all these names and forms of judicial organization at once. Gradually, you'll develop a sensitivity to these matters as you read cases from different states.

THE MEANING OF ALL THE ITEMS AT THE BEGINNING OF THE CASE

The caption of the case:

McBoyle v. United States

At the trial level, the order was reversed: the indictment by the federal jury read *The United States v. McBoyle* and that was the title of the trial proceeding because the federal government, not a private individual, was prosecuting McBoyle. Criminal prosecutions are carried out by the federal or state governments. Criminal law is public law, not private law. The parties are the state and the defendant, not the complainant (the victim) and the defendant. From our prior discussion, you may know why McBoyle's name goes first in the caption of the case. He was the petitioner in the United States Supreme Court; he had been granted a review by the Court of his claim of legal error committed by the United States Court of Appeals (10th Cir.). Another frequently used label to describe McBoyle's position is the "appellant."

The citation of the case:

283 U.S. 25 (1931)

This is the official citation for the *McBoyle* case in the United States Supreme Court. It means that this opinion is reported in Volume 283 of the United States Reports, the official, court-authorized system for reporting the cases decided by the Supreme Court. These cases are published by the Government Printing Office in Washington, D.C. The number "25" refers to the initial page on which the case is printed.

Docket and dates:

No. 552 Argued February 26, 27, 1931 - Decided March 9, 1931

The "No. 522" refers simply to the Supreme Court docket number for this case, and the rest refers to the dates of oral argument by the lawyers before the Court and the official date of decision and publication of the opinion.

The headnote:

> The National Motor Vehicle Theft Act, U.S.C., Title 18, re P. 39 §408, which punishes whoever transports, or causes to be transported, in interstate or foreign commerce a motor vehicle knowing it to have been stolen, and which defines "motor vehicle" as including "an automobile, automobile truck, automobile wagon, motor cycle, or any other self-propelled vehicle not designed for running on rails," does not apply to aircraft. P. 26.

> 43 F. (2d) 273, reversed.

I suggest scanning such headnotes but not concentrating on them. A headnote is a brief summary of the issues decided in a case, including the important facts. A headnote is not part of the court's opinion. It is added by the Reporter of Decisions or by the editor of the volume.

The citation, "43 F. (2d) 273, reversed," refers to the reversal by the Supreme Court of the judgment of the U.S. Court of Appeals (10th Cir.) which is reported in 43 F.2d 273, the forty-third volume of the Federal Reported (an official system for reporting federal court cases other than Supreme Court cases) on page 273.

The citation "43 F. (2d) 273, reversed," refers to the reversal by the Supreme Court of the Judgment of the U.S. Court of Appeals (10th Cir.) which is reported in 43 F. 2d 273, the forty-third volume of the Federal Reporter (an official system for reporting federal court cases other than Supreme Court cases) on page 273.

Next, beneath the headnote:

> CERTIORARI, 282 U.S. 835, to review a judgment affirming a conviction under the Motor Vehicle Theft Act.

You should be able to understand what this means. If not, please refer to my prior definition of the "writ of certiorari" (p. 38). The citation "282 U.S. 835" refers to the official report of the Supreme Court's decision on the preliminary proceeding by McBoyle asking the Court, in its discretion, to agree to hear and decide his claim of legal error. It reads:

> No. 552. *McBoyle v. United States.* January 12, 1931.
> Petition for writ of certiorari to the Circuit Court of Appeals for the Tenth Circuit granted, limited to the question whether the National Motor Vehicle Theft Act applies to aircraft. Mr. Harry F. Brown for petitioner, Solicitor General Thacher and Messrs. Claude R. Branch, Harry S. Ridgely, and W. Marvin Smith for the United States. Reported below: 43 F (2d) 273.

Last, you see the following:

> Mr. Harry F. Brown for Petitioner.

> Mr. Claude R. Branch, Special Assistant to the Attorney General, with whom Solicitor General Thacher, Assistant Attorney General Dodds and Messrs. Harry S. Ridgely and W. Marvin Smith were on the brief, for the United States.

As may be apparent to you, Brown is the attorney who represented McBoyle in the Supreme Court. The other names refer to the government lawyers who represented the United States in the Supreme Court on this case.

While you concentrate in briefing and in class discussion on the court's opinion, you should be aware of the meaning of these preliminary matters.

CHAPTER

THREE

INTRODUCTION

Applying what you have learned about briefing in the prior chapter, brief the following case in contracts. Use the six-step approach and apply the guidelines as demonstrated in the prior chapter. Two particular challenges are presented by this case.

First, you may have to struggle to understand the facts. As in many cases, they are somewhat complicated. For those of you with some business background, you may be able to understand the facts after two or three meticulous readings. For those many of you without such background, understanding these facts may require many meticulous readings, aided by Black's Law Dictionary and by Webster's English Dictionary. There is no escape from this effort: cases present fact situations from commerce and virtually every other area of life. Some fact patterns will be simple and clear as in *McBoyle*; many others will be complicated and unfamiliar, depending on your academic and work experience. One consolation: gradually you acquire an understanding of commercial and other fact patterns which initially may be quite strange. Remember, cases pivot on their facts: you must become fact-centered or, if you prefer, fact-obsessed.

Second, this court opinion includes varied types of legal reasoning. Your briefing challenge is to demonstrate that you understand the opinion by being able to identify, categorize, and succinctly present these varied types of legal reasoning. Your struggling to do so is a fundamental part of your learning of the basic skills.

PORT HURON MACHINERY COMPANY, LIMITED, Appellee, v. FRED WOHLERS, Appellant.

***

Appeal from Des Moines Municipal Court.—J. E. MERSHON, Judge.

NOVEMBER 13, 1928.

REHEARING DENIED FEBRUARY 15, 1929.

Action at law, to recover liquidated damages, as stipulated in an alleged written contract or order for the purchase of certain farm machinery by the defendant (appellant) from the plaintiff. The defendant in answer admits that he signed the written order for purchase of the goods, and that he refused the shipment of the goods, but pleads an oral condition precedent, to wit: That the goods were to be delivered on or before a certain date, and that, by reason of his cancellation of the order before delivery, and before notification of acceptance of the order by plaintiff, an enforcible contract did not result. No evidence was introduced by the defendant. Upon the conclusion of the introduction of plaintiff's testimony, the defendant moved the court to instruct the jury to return a verdict for the defendant. This motion was overruled, and thereupon the plaintiff moved the court to instruct the jury to return a verdict for the plaintiff. This motion was sustained, and the jury was directed to return a verdict for the plaintiff in the sum of $349.55. Judgment was entered in conformity to the verdict, and the defendant appeals.—*Affirmed.*

Havens & Elston, for appellant.

Strock, Cunningham, Sloan & Herrick, for appellee.

DE GRAFF, J.—This case involves an alleged contract containing a stipulation for liquidated damages. If a contract did result, there can be no question that the plaintiff is entitled to recover, since the terms of the alleged contract clearly fix the amount recoverable by plaintiff in case of a breach. See *Pace v. Zellmer,* 194 Iowa 516.

This appeal presents but one question. It is a question of law, and calls for the statement of the applicable legal principle. But, like every other case, the governing principle arises out of a fact situation. It is said in *Steffes v. Hale,* 204 Iowa 226:

"It is almost a legal maxim that 'out of the facts the law arises,' since, if there be no state of facts, there can be no question of law."

We necessarily first turn to the factual side.

On July 18, 1927, a written order signed by the defendant was delivered to plaintiff's agent, and in that order the plaintiff was directed to deliver immediately, or as soon thereafter as possible, to the defendant on board cars, consigned to the order of plaintiff, at Neola, Iowa, defendant's place of residence, certain described goods (farm machinery) . The order further states that the defendant will receive the machinery, pay the freight charges, and also pay to the plaintiff, on or before the arrival of the machinery, the sum of $1,562.50, in the manner and form recited in the order. Further:

"If, for any reason, the purchaser fails to accept and settle for the machinery order, he will, if the company so elects and demands, pay to the company, in lieu of the enforcement of this contract, as liquidated damages, a sum equal to ten per cent to the list price, and, if shipment has been made, freight from the factory and return, demurrage, cartage, loading and unloading expense and all other similar expenses actually incurred by reason of the shipment and attempted delivery of said machinery; if suit is commenced to enforce the performance of any part of this contract the purchaser agrees to pay a reasonable attorney's fee."

The plaintiff's agent immediately, upon the signing of this order by defendant, telephoned the plaintiff at Des Moines the receipt of the order, and requested that the goods be loaded and sent forthwith to the defendant. On July 20,1927, the plaintiff filled the order in accordance with its terms, and shipped the goods. On July 22, 1927, the plaintiff received a telegram from the defendant, bearing date July 21st, which said: "Delivery date specified on thresher deal now past and order is hereby cancelled." The plaintiff, as a result of defendant's attempt to revoke and cancel the order, and his refusal to accept the goods, was obliged to recall the goods and reship them to the point of delivery, thereby incurring certain expense, which was established by competent proof upon the trial of this case. True, the defendant in his answer alleged a condition precedent, but the allegation continued to rest in the answer. It finds no support in the evidence. When the plaintiff rested its case, motions for a directed verdict were made respectively by the parties. The plaintiff's motion was sustained. The question, therefore, at this point is whether the plaintiff established a prima-facie case. The contention of the defendant on appeal is that the plaintiff failed to prove a contract, for the reason that there is no showing that the plaintiff accepted the offer of the defendant and communicated the acceptance of the offer prior to its revocation by the defendant.

The point is now reached that we may discuss the law involved, under the undisputed facts. Did a contract result? It is not practicable, nor is it necessary, in a definition of contract, to state all of the operative facts or all of the legal relations that are created by such facts. contract may be deemed as a promise, the performance of which the law recognizes as a duty, and for a breach of which a remedy is given. A contract, therefore, does not contemplate simply the act of promising, but obligations arising therefrom. The law recognizes, as a matter of classification, two kinds of contracts,—unilateral and bilateral. In the case at bar, a typical example of unilateral contract is found, since it s universally agreed that a unilateral contract is one in which no promisor receives a promise as consideration; whereas, in a bilateral contract, there are mutual promises between the two parties to the contract. This matter of definition has recently received careful consideration by the American Law Institute, and may be found in the Restatement of the Law of Contracts, Proposed Final Draft No. 1 (April 18,1928),17, Section 12. In the instant case, the offer of the defendant must be viewed as a promise. It is promissory in terms. The rule is well stated by Professor Williston: A promise which the promisor should reasonably expect to induce action or forbearance of a definite and substantial character on the part of the promisee, and which does induce such action or forbearance, is binding if injustice can be avoided only by enforcement of the promise. See 1 Williston on Contracts, Section 139. Clearly, the instant offer, signed by the defendant, was of this character. Appellant, however, contends that there was no acceptance of the offer. Words are not the only medium of expression of mutual assent. An offer may invite an acceptance to be made by merely an affirmative answer, or by performing a specific act. True, if an act other than a promise is requested, no contract exists until what is requested is performed or tendered, in whole or in part. We are here dealing with a unilateral contract, and the act requested and performed as consideration for the contract indicates acceptance, as well as furnishes the consideration. The sending of an order for goods to a merchant is an offer of a promise for an act. 13 Corpus Juris 266, Section 57. In the same text it is said that an acceptance of an offer may be by acts, as where an offer is made that the offerer will pay or do something else, if the offeree shall do a particular thing. In such a case, performance is the only thing needful to complete the agreement and to create a binding promise. Ibid. 275, Section 73. It must be kept in mind that there is a distinction in regard to communication of acceptance between offers which ask that the offeree *shall do* something, as in the instant case, and offers which ask that the offeree *shall promise* something. In offers of the latter kind, communication of the acceptance is always essential. Ibid. 284, 285, Sections 88, 89.

The decisions of this court are in accord with the general rule. In *Hankins v. Young,* 174 Iowa 383, it is said:

"In the case of an order for goods, the delivery of the goods in pursuance of the order is an acceptance of the order."

To the same effect is *Petroleum Prod. Distributing Co. v. Alton Tank Line,* 165 Iowa 398; *Rock Island Plow Co. v. Meredith,* 107 Iowa 498; *McCormick Harv. Mach. Co. v. Markert,* 107 Iowa 340. Pertinent language is used in *McCormick Harv. Mach. Co. v. Richardson,* 89 Iowa 525, wherein it is said:

"We do not say that the acceptance must be a formal one. The acceptance might be shown by proving an act done on the faith of the order. such as the shipment of the goods ordered."

An especially clear expression of the rule is found in *McDermott v. Mahoney,* 139 Iowa 292, wherein the written instrument was recognized and held to be a unilateral contract, as it was signed by one party only, and by him delivered to the other, and accepted as a contract between the parties. It is said:

"Where a written agreement signed by one party is accepted and adopted by the other, and acted upon, it becomes their contract, in the same sense as though both. parties had signed it."

See, also, *Reynolds v. Johnson,* 199 Iowa 1055.

A typical case adopting the same rule is *Kingman & Co. v. Watson,* 97 Wis. 596 (73 N. W. 438). .See, also, notes in 19 A. L. R. 476 and 29 A. L. R. 1352.

Certain cases are cited by appellant in brief, but they are distinguishable from the case at bar on the fact side. For instance: In *Thompson & Sons Mfg. Co. v. Perkins & Son,* 97 Iowa 607, the order was given in November, 1892, for goods to be shipped February 14, 1893. The offeree made no acceptance, either formal or by shipment, and, two weeks before shipment date, the offer was revoked. The revocation was held legally permissible, under the facts. The same is true in *Hargrove v. Crawford,* 159 Iowa 522; *Durkee v. Schultz,* 122 Iowa 410; *Doll & Smith v. A. & S. San. Dairy Co.,* 202 Iowa 786.

The instant appeal primarily has an educational value. The applicable legal principle is well settled, on both reason and authority. The judgment entered by the trial court is—*Affirmed.*

STEVENS, C. J., and ALBERT, MORLING, and WAGNER, JJ., concur.

Contrast your brief with the following excellent brief. Language can vary, including method of expression and abbreviation. That is not critical. What is critical is to demonstrate a clear grasp of the facts, the procedural history, the precise issue in controversy, the holding and judgment, and an understanding of the reasoning. As you study this excellent brief, please reflect on my comments on the left.

Port Huron Mach.Co. v Wohlers
207 Iowa 826 (1928)
221 NW 843

FACTS

A) D-buyer delivered written order to P-seller's agent on 7/18/27 directing P to deliver farm machinery to D at Neola, Iowa.

B) The order also specified that if b/k by D-B, specified liquidated damages would be paid to P-S.

C) P-seller's A immed., upon receipt of signed order called P-S at Des Moines & requested that machinery be loaded & sent to D-B. Shipped 7/20 per D-B's order to Neola, Iowa.

D) On 7/22, P-S received D-B's telegram, "Delivery date specified on thresher deal now past & order is hereby cancelled."

E) D-B refused shipment. P-S initiated c/a for money for b/k (offer, acceptance, consideration & breach). D-B argued on appeal than no K existed because P-S never **accepted** D-B's offer before D-B revoked his offer.

At trial, the seller was the plaintiff (P) and the buyer was the defendant (D). The appellate court used the same labels in its opinion. It helps to refer to the P-S (plaintiff-seller) and to the D-B (defendant-buyer). The case determined the rights and liabilities of a P-S and a D-B.

Note the step-by-step breakdown of the facts.

This segment specifies P-S's cause-of-action against D-B and the elements of that c/a. This segment also specifies D-B's defense that no K existed because there was no acceptance. This statement of facts pinpoints element in controversy on appeal: the acceptance necessary for a K.

PROCEDURAL HISTORY

At end of P-S's case (i.e., the introduction of P-S's evidence) in trial court, both sides rested. D-B's motion for directed verdict for D-B rejected. P-S's motion for directed verdict for P-S granted for $349.55. Judgment entered for P-S. D-B appeals.

This statement of the procedural history pinpoints the exact disposition in the trial court and thus aids in pinpointing the issue in controversy to be resolved on appeal.

ISSUE

Whether the P-S's shipment of the machinery, as requested by D's order, constituted the acceptance necessary for a unilateral K?

A neutral, precise and hence preferable issue-formulation.

Again, this holding was implied or implicit, rather than being directly stated with words such as "we hold...."

HOLDING

Yes. For a unilateral contract, acceptance of the offer was demonstrated by performance of the requested act—here the shipping of the machinery. (No acceptance in the form of a promise was necessary.)

The result or disposition here in the appellate court for the P-S affirmed the trial court result.

JUDGMENT

Judgment at trial ct. f/P-S affirmed.

REASONING

The court's reasoning is unusual because of its pedagogic style: a systematic presentation of the basic rules of contract law. Most court opinions are not comparably pedagogic on the convincing ground that cases are designed for decision of controversies, not for teaching law students. Hence, most, if not all, of this initial presentation of basic rules should be omitted, even though it is both true and fundamental, because it was not necessary to detail it to decide the appeal.

There was a unilateral K: an act was requested by D-B and performed by P-S; P's shipping of the machinery was both:
—acceptance &
—consideration

As C.J. states: the sending of an order of goods to a merchant is an offer of a promise for an act. D's order was an offer and P's shipping of goods was acceptance and consideration. Performance, as here, completed the agreement and created a binding promise (a K).

There are two kinds of offers:
A) as here, P's offer asking D to do something (ship mach.)
B) an offer asking other party to promise something.

Corpus Juris (C.J.) is a legal encyclopedia, a comprehensive restatement in text form of American Law, topic by topic. Like the court's use of Professor Williston's analysis, Corpus Juris is another example of **persuasive authority.** *Though often cited, it is not legally binding. Interweaving of key facts and elements of offer, acceptance & consideration necessary for a K.*

If latter, commun. of acceptance is essential.

In contrast to the persuasive authority of Professor Williston and Corpus Juris, the holdings of the court in its prior cases with similar facts and issues are **binding authority;** *such holdings must be followed by the court in the instant case (see p.5)*

Ct. cites its prior decisions, *Hawkins v. Young:* "In the case of an order for goods, the delivery of goods" per order "is an acceptance of order"; *McDermott v. Mahoney:* Where a written agreement signed by 1 party is accept. and adopt. by other, and acted upon, it becomes their K. as though both parties had signed it.

The citation to a Wisconsin case and to the American Law Reports *are additional examples of the Courts use of* **persuasive authority.** *The* American Law Reports *(ALR) is a digest of relevant cases, statutes and regulations, organized topic by topic.*

Also in accord: a Wis. case and ALR

The cases cited by the D-B in support of his defense were rejected by the court. Why? The facts in those cases were <u>not</u> *similar to the facts of this case. Hence, the holdings in those cases were not applicable here. They are precedents which did* <u>not</u> <u>control</u> *this case.*

Cases cited by appellant were **factually distinguishable**— e.g. in *Thompson v. Perkins,* the offer (order) was never accepted (no shipment was made).

Comment

Did you notice that this brief is entitled **An Excellent Beginner's Brief**? Why? In the first few weeks of studying contracts, you are just learning the most basic rules of contracts. Hence, your detailing in the reasoning segment of your brief of some of these rules is justified; it helps you to learn them. After some weeks, however, there is no need for this detail even if the opinion contains it. Indeed, most opinions will short-circuit, or even presuppose, much of what the court here has specified. With experience and confidence, your reasoning segment could be presented as follows.

REASONING

For a unilateral K., the performance of the act requested in an offer constitutes the acceptance. D-B's order was an offer and P-S's performance of the act requested, shipment of farm machinery, was acceptance (& consideration). K results.

Authority

Binding: Ct.'s prior decisions: *Hawkins v. Young:* "deliv. of goods" pursuant to an order is an "accept. of order." Also in accord: *McDermott v. Mahoney*

Persuasive: Williston: C.J.; ALR

D's cases distinguishable on facts: no shipment made.

Remember: If K had been bilateral, then promise needed for acceptance.

The advantage of this more succinct recitation of the court's reasoning is not simply a saving of time. It is also a demonstration of focus: you pinpoint the heart of the reasoning—the reason why your professor has assigned this case. Such pinpointing takes time—and much briefing. (Incidentally, it is also possible here, with experience and confidence, to state the facts more succinctly.)

Nevertheless, it's a mistake in the very beginning to attempt this degree of succinctness. Why? It presupposes what you do not have—the skills to pinpoint the essence of the reasoning. Hence, rather than being succinct, you risk being cryptic, missing important aspects of the reasoning.

A POOR BRIEF

As you study this brief, your objectives are:

- to understand exactly the defects in this brief and why these defects are wrong
- to search for defects illustrated here which you are committing, and
- hence, to avoid these mistakes

Lacks date and citation

The mistakes here are:
- *recitation of facts lacks concreteness*
- *it does not specify who is the P and who is the D (the P-S and the D-B).*

It's a mistake to quote extensively from the opinion. The errors of so doing are prolixity and a substitute for trying to identify and understand the key facts.

It's wrong to say D cancelled his order. It's correct to say D attempted to cancel his order.

Just a quotation from case: no indication that student understands any of this. Incorporating the procedural history in the fact step is all right in principle but it is poorly done here—no clear statement of procedural history (who won judgment in trial court?, who is appealing?)

Port Huron Mach. Co. v. Wohlers

FACTS

These facts relate to a sale of goods by seller to buyer. The seller apparently solicited the buyer to purchase the goods. The buyer placed an order with the seller to deliver the goods. Buyer agreed to pay $1562.50 for goods. Buyer's order also stated:

> "If, for any reason, the purchaser fails to accept and settle for the machinery order, he will, if the company so elects and demands, pay to the company, in lieu of the enforcement of this contract, as liquidated damages, a sum equal to ten per cent of the list price, and, if shipment has been made, freight from the factory and return, demurrage, cartage, loading and unloading expenses and all other similar expenses actually incurred by reason of the shipment and attempted deliver of said machinery; if the suit is commenced to enforce the performance of any part of this contract the purchaser agrees to pay a reasonable attorney's fee."

The order was shipped on July 20, 1927. The D, however, sent a telegram on 7/21, delivered on 7/22, cancelling his order:

> "Delivery date specified on thresher deal now past and order is hereby cancelled."

P incurred costs in reshipping the goods.

> "True, the defendant in his answer alleged a condition precedent, but the allegation continued to rest in the answer. It finds no support in the evidence. When the plaintiff rested its case, motions for a directed verdict were made respectively by the parties. The plaintiff's motion was sustained."

ISSUE

a) The issue is whether the P failed to prove the existence of a K because there was no showing that the P accepted the offer of the D and communicated the acceptance of said offer; <u>or</u>

b) As stated by the court: "the question…is whether the P established a **prima facie** case."

Wrong. Notice that this articulation of the issue from the case explicitly presents the D's formulation ("The contention of the defendant on appeal is…")

Wrong. Even though the court articulated the issue in this form, it is incorrect for you to use it. Its defects are:
• it inquires solely about a legal conclusion (a prima facie case)
• it is too broad (it does not focus on the exact legal question posed by the facts)
• it fails to include any key facts from the instant fact situation. See preferable statement of issues on p. 19)

HOLDING

The holding is that P established a **prima facie** case and deserved the liquidated damages.

Wrong. A broad formulation of the issue leads to a broad formulation of the holding which could apply to many cases, not only this one. It also lacks any reference to instant key facts. Remember: a holding (and an issue) incorporates applicable rule and key facts to which it applies.

REASONING

As the court stated, "the governing principle arises out of a fact situation…":

> It is almost a legal maxim "out of the facts the law arises, since, if there be no state of facts, there can be no question of law."

This sentence expresses a profound, underlying legal truth. A brief of a case, however, is not the place for such a statement, unless it illumines the holding (or issue, or statement of key facts).

The court then discussed two conceptions of a K. The first conception of a K is:

> a promise, the performance of which the law recognizes as a duty and for a breach of which a remedy is given.

The second conception of Professor Williston:

> a promise which the promisor would reasonably expect to induce action or forbearance of a definite and substantial character on the part of the promisee, and which does induce such action or forbearance, is binding if injustice can be avoided only by enforcement of the promise

What is significant is the legal reasoning which specifically explains and justifies the court's decision-making. In a brief, therefore, you concentrate on such reasoning. This exposition of the court's reasoning does not so concentrate. It also offends another precept of case briefing—conciseness. Gradually you develop judgment in distinguishing this type of introductory exposition of basic rules from the legal reasoning which directly supports the holding.

In addition, the court stressed that the law recognizes two kinds of contracts: a bilateral contract and, as here, a unilateral contract.

In contrast to the above detail, an explanation of the difference between the two types of contracts is not specified. A clear understanding of this difference is essential to understand the case.

The first sentence is a masterpiece of confusion:
a) it presupposes what is to be decided—whether or not there was a contract
b) it mistakenly confuses the parties—the D at trial was the appellant on this appeal. The P at trial was the appellee on this appeal. In this opinion, the court mostly used the trial labels—the seller was the P, the buyer was the D.

There was a prima facie case here because the appellant performed the obligation imposed on him by the contract. The contract here was a unilateral contract and hence the performance by the appellant established the consideration (and incidentally the acceptance) which was necessary. Professor Williston, as a learned commentator, and especially his famous book on contracts, plus *Corpus Juris*, a well-known legal encyclopedia, provided the necessary authority for these basic legal policies.

Performance of the delivery of the machinery was the acceptance (which is not incidental) and the consideration.

Professor Williston and the Corpus Juris *did not provide the necessary legal authority: they provided* **persuasive authority,** *not* **binding authority.**

The court's opinion set forth basic rules or principles, not policies.

There is no indication that the student knows that these prior precedents were binding on the court in the instant case.

In addition, there was other legal authority for this statement of law. See, e.g., *Hawkins v. Young*; and

Do not include a string of citations.

"*Petroleum Products Distribution Co. v. Alton Tank Line,* 165 Iowa 398, 146 N.W. 52; *Rock Island Plow Co. v. Meredith,* 107 Iowa 498, 78 N.W. 233; *McCormick Harvesting Machines Co. V. Markert,* 107 Iowa 340, 78 N.W. 33. Pertinent language is used in *McCormick Harvesting Machine Co. v. Richardson.*"

Abbreviations would save valuable time.

In *McDermott v. Mahoney*, the court, e.g., said:

"Where a written agreement signed by one party is accepted and adopted by the other, and acted upon, it becomes their contract in the same sense as though both parties had signed it."

This distinguishing was on the facts—and that should be specified.	The court then distinguished a series of other cases from the instant case. These included:

> *Hargrove v. Crawford*, 159 Iowa 522, 141 N.W. 423: *Durkee v. Schultz*, 122 Iowa 410, 98 N.W. 149; *Doll & Smith v. A.& S. Sanitary Diary Co.*, 202 Iowa 786, 211 N.W. 230.

Judgment for whom?   Judgment of trial court affirmed.

FUNCTION OF THE COURT EXEMPLIFIED IN PORT HURON

In *McBoyle* in Chapter II, the U.S. Supreme Court exemplified one of its functions—acting as the final judicial arbiter of a claim of error arising from a dispute over the meaning of a federal statute as applied to a particular fact situation. Here, in *Port Huron*, the function exemplified by the Supreme Court of Iowa is deciding a claim of error committed by the trial court arising from the application of a certain common law rule of contract to the instant fact situation. In contrast to *McBoyle,* where the claimed legal error arose from the trial court's application of a federal statute, the claim of error in *Port Huron* arises not from a rule based in a statute, but rather from a rule rooted in case law. There is not a single reference in *Port Huron* to any statute. What the Iowa Supreme Court did in *Port Huron* is one function performed by appellate courts every day: deciding appeals which urge claims of legal error based on the application by the trial court of particular rules rooted in cases and resulting judge-made precedent.

Comment

I recognize that, as a beginner, studying and briefing *Port Huron* could easily take you a number of hours. Don't be discouraged—this is entirely normal in the beginning. In addition, don't be discouraged if you are confused and make mistakes—this too is entirely to be expected. Indeed, it is essential. You clarify your understanding of cases by gradually dispelling the swirling mist of confusion. In this quest for understanding of appellate cases, you are doing exercises in legal reasoning. Consciously and subconsciously, bit by bit, you are developing your basic skills in:

- extricating key facts

- issue spotting and specification

- selecting rules

- applying rules to facts, especially by interweaving

- adroitly using policy (not in *Port Huron*)

- lawyerly writing

RELEVANCE FOR LAWYERING

As you struggle, it might encourage you if you clearly appreciate the relevance of what you are doing for actual lawyering. In practice, for example, a common question from a judge (at motion, trial or appellate levels) is—"What does X case stand for?" If X case is *Port Huron*, cited in oral argument or written brief, your reply might be:

> *Port Huron* affirms the principle that for a unilateral contract the performance of the act requested in the offer is sufficient to establish acceptance.

This response is direct, precise and, therefore, lawyerly. To be able to boil down *Port Huron* in this way, your basic skills must be honed by briefing, classroom discussion, writing, etc. Remember the story of the French Impressionist painter who was challenged in a lawsuit over the fairness of a two-thousand-dollar price for a sketch he completed in two minutes. His reply: it required thirty-five years to learn how to do the sketch in two minutes. It may well take you hours to be able to boil *Port Huron* down to its legal essence. Take heart: what requires hours in the beginning will require a fraction of this time after your basic skills are sharpened.

THE PRINCIPLE OF *PORT HURON*

Some judges, and some first-year professors, will not ask "what does *Port Huron* stand for?" but rather will ask "what is the principle affirmed by *Port Huron*?" The response is the same as to the first question. In this identical response to the two questions, you have omitted the specific illustration of "performance of the act requested in the offer," i.e., the plaintiff-seller's shipment of the farm machinery in *Port Huron*. That specific shipment is central to pinpointing the issue in controversy and the holding in *Port Huron*. Nevertheless, in responding to the hypothetical judge's question, or your professor's question, about the principle of *Port Huron*, you omit the fact of the shipment. What was critical to the formulation of the issue and holding in *Port Huron*, is now omitted as a mere illustration. Why? The answer is that the judge and your professor are not asking about the issue and holding in *Port Huron*. Instead, their questions inquire about the principle which underlies this issue and holding. In understanding this principle, *Port Huron* becomes only an example of its application and the shipment of the farm machinery only one of many possible illustrations of it.

THE *RATIO DECIDENDI*

Some first year professors, but not judges, will also inquire of you about the *ratio decidendi* of a court's holding and judgment. That generally means a more general legal standard, either a principle or possibly a policy, which both underlies and compels the holding judgment. Stated differently, it is that part of the court's reasoning absolutely required for its holding. Indeed, some first-year professors require you to include the *ratio decidendi* in the statement of the holding. In *Port Huron*, the *ratio decidendi* is clearly identical with the principle set forth above. In many cases, however, the *ratio decidendi* is not clear. Indeed, the waters are murky here in the use of *ratio decidendi* and the principle of a case. Don't expect scientific-type clarity. Do follow your professor's usage in each course.

DICTA

This culminating skill in catching the legal essence of a case also aids you in understanding the holding-dicta distinction. The **holding** here in response to the issue raised by the key facts is what the case has authoritatively decided. This is the law of the case. This is the precedent which triggers the application of ***stare decisis*** for future cases with similar facts and issues. This only is what the court has the power to decide, the particular issue in controversy which is before the court, and nothing else. When the holding is new, the court makes new law, judge-made law.. When, as in *Port Huron*, the holding does not announce new law, it affirms an existing rule or principle of law.

In contrast, all reasoning which is not necessary for the holding is **dicta**. It may be undeniable, basic rules and maxims of law—e.g., the introductory explanation in *Port Huron* that "out of the facts the law arises;" and the initial pedagogic review of basic contract rules. The point is not that dicta is necessarily unimportant. The point is that dicta in a case has a different legal status and consequence from the case holding. Dicta is not the law of the case and is not controlling for future cases with similar facts and issues.

HOLDINGS

For many beginning students, learning the importance of case holdings leads to a typical first-year blunder: an obsession with holdings to the detriment of the key facts and the issues which led to the holdings and without which the holdings are **legally meaningless**. The utter fallacy inherent in this obsession should be apparent to you if you remember that the learning of legal reasoning is the *raison d'être* of the first year.

Issues not considered and decided in *Port Huron*

Again, it may shed light to consider some of the many issues which were not considered and decided in *Port Huron* and to understand exactly why such issues were not considered and decided. These include the following:

Issue	Why not considered
Whether the defendant-buyer's claim that he cancelled his order (the offer necessary for a contract) was valid?	*While this claim was advanced in the defendant's answer (a pre-trial pleading), the defendant at trial introduced "no evidence" at all. Ordinarily, an appellate court may not consider or decide an issue not considered and decided at trial. Ordinarily, an appellate court has no power to consider issues in the first instance ("de novo"), to receive evidence, and to decide them. Trial courts perform these tasks.*
Whether the defendant had a good motive for trying (unsuccessfully) to cancel the contract?	*Not a legal issue. Underlying motive is legally irrelevant here.*
Whether the defendant's decision at trial to "introduce no evidence" was wise?	*Not a legal issue for trial or appellate court. Lawyers determine trial strategy and tactics*
Whether the price of $1562.50 for the farm machinery was ethically justified?	*Not a legal issue. Courts decide legal issues, not ethical issues.*
Whether the price of $1562.50 was economically justified?	*Not a legal issue. Courts decide legal issues, not economic issues.*
Whether the Supreme Court of Iowa should have referred this case back to the trial court with a recommendation that the plaintiff and defendant reach a negotiated settlement, or failing that, they relitigate the facts and law.	*Improper. Not the role of an appellate court. An appellate court (and a trial court) must decide the controversy presented to it by the parties (plaintiff and defendant). It may not decline to decide because it would prefer a negotiated settlement or because it regards judicial decision-making as unwise or difficult.* *Moreover, an appellate court has no power to order a relitigation of the factual and legal issued decided at trial unless it finds legal error by the trial court which compels reversal or modification of the trial court.*

MORE DEFINITIONS

Prima Facie Case (at first view)—very simply means that the plaintiff must introduce sufficient evidence at trial to establish the plaintiff's cause-of-action if it is assumed that such evidence is true and credible. Only then will the judge allow the case to go to the jury for fact-finding. Slightly elaborated, it means that the plaintiff at trial must introduce sufficient facts (e.g., testimony, documents, and "order for goods") which prove, if believed, each element of the legal claim asserted, so that the trial judge is satisfied that the jury could reasonably find a verdict for the plaintiff. The trial judge alone determines whether or not a **prima facie** case has been established. Sometimes, the **prima facie** case is called the **burden of production** (of producing evidence). In *Port Huron*, the plaintiff-seller introduced evidence (a written order and testimony) to prove that the plaintiff-seller and the defendant-buyer entered into a contract and that the defendant breached the contract, entitling the plaintiff to money damages. The plaintiff's **prima facie** case consisted of evidence to prove the elements of a contract (refusal to accept delivery of the machinery), and damages (specified liquidated damages, freight charges, etc.).

Burden of Proof—has two meanings. The first relates to the plaintiff's burden of proving a *prima facie* case.

Once the trial judge determines that a *prima facie* case has been established, the plaintiff, or prosecutor in a criminal case, then has a second challenge: to persuade the fact-finder (judge or jury) that all the evidence introduced at trial proves the legal claim asserted by the standard of a preponderance of the evidence (civil case) or by the standard of beyond a reasonable doubt (criminal case). This is the second and more usual meaning of burden of proof. It is also called the **burden of persuasion.** In *Port Huron*, a civil case, the breach of contract must be proved by a preponderance of the evidence.

Directed Verdict—when the trial judge directs a verdict for one party against the other party. A motion for a directed verdict should be granted if all the evidence (the facts and inferences) "point so strongly and overwhelmingly in favor of one party the Court [judge] believes that reasonable men could not arrive at a contrary verdict...." (*Boeing Co. v. Shipman*, 411 F.2d 365, 374 [5th Cir. 1969]). In considering whether or not to grant such a motion, a trial court must consider "all of the evidence..." from the standpoint "most favorable" to the party against whom the motion is made. In criminal cases, however, there can be no directed verdict against the defendant.

In *Port Huron*, the trial court granted the plaintiff-seller's motion for a directed verdict in its favor. The trial court apparently decided that since the defendant-buyer introduced "no evidence" at trial, there was no factual issue presented for the jury to decide. The only matter remaining was the application of a clear legal rule: for a unilateral contract, acceptance may be established by performance of the requested act. The trial court applied this rule to the undisputed facts and the result was clear. By granting the plaintiff's motion for a directed verdict, the trial court implicitly stated that no reasonable juror could find to the contrary. In rejecting the defendant-buyer's claim of legal error because of this directed verdict, the appellate court, the Supreme Court of Iowa, affirmed the legal correctness of the trial court's granting of the motion for a directed verdict for the plaintiff.

Complaint—in a common meaning in a civil case, a complaint is a formal written pleading by which a plaintiff initiates a legal proceeding against a defendant. A complaint asserts a legal claim, often called a **cause-of-action**, alleging a violation of a legal right of the plaintiff by the defendant. A complaint demands a remedy for this claimed violation. In *Port Huron*, the plaintiff-seller initiated a legal proceeding against the defendant-buyer with a complaint which alleged that the defendant-buyer breached his contractual duty owed to the plaintiff-seller by refusing to accept and pay for the farm machinery. For this claimed breach of contract, the plaintiff-seller demanded money damages as specified in the contract.

Answer—has many different meanings as used in cases. One of these meanings is a pre-trial pleading by a defendant in a civil case: an answer is a written response to the plaintiff's allegations in a complaint, setting forth the legal and factual allegations which comprise the basis of the defense. In *Port Huron*, this was the meaning of the court's use of the word: "(t)he defendant in his answer...but the allegation continued to rest in the answer." This word "answer" is an example of the use in opinions of words which have a common English meaning and a particular legal meaning (see p. 10).

Contract—a simple, much-quoted definition of a contract is set forth in the American Law Institute's *Restatement of the Law of Contracts* (§ 1):

> A contract is a promise or a set of promises for the breach of which the law gives a remedy, or the performance of which the law in some way recognizes as a duty.

Promisor—a person who makes a promise.

Promisee—a person to whom a promise is made.

Promise—has multiple meanings, like so many words used in cases. Its particular meaning must, therefore, be determined with each use. In the *Restatement of the Law of Contracts* (§ 2), a promise is defined as follows:

> …a manifestation of intention to act or refrain from acting in a specified way, so made as to justify a promisee in understanding that a commitment has been made.

American Law Institute—An independent, private, law-reform organization composed of American judges, lawyers and professors who prepare model legislative codes in many areas of law for consideration by the various state legislatures. For example, the Institute's *Model Penal Code* has influenced many legislative recodifications of state penal codes. Its *Uniform Commercial Code* has been adopted in most states. Its Restatements of Law (e.g., Torts, Contracts, Property) describe what the current state of law is in a particular area and specify changes that should take place, in the judgment of the American Law Institute. Courts often adopt Restatement principles.

Public and **Private Law**—In public law, as illustrated by *McBoyle*, in the last chapter, the state is a party to the criminal law action. Indeed, the criminal indictment is brought in the name of the "United States of America" against McBoyle, the defendant. In contrast, in private law, as illustrated by *Port Huron* in this chapter, the parties to the action for damages for breach of contract are private, the Port Huron Machinery Company and Fred Wohler. The state is <u>not</u> a part to the action.

The animating theory of private law, exemplified in the model of contracts, is that the private parties make their own private law, the agreement of the parties, and embody it in a contract. If a dispute erupts between the parties, the role of the civil courts is to enforce this private law, <u>if</u> the contract has been formed in accordance with the authorizing rules (e.g., offer, acceptance, consideration), and in accordance with such other rules as capacity (e.g., infancy, incompetency), the statute of frauds (e.g., real property transfers) and avoidance of fraud and unconscionability.

What confuses some students is the impact of the enforcing role of the court on the public/private law distinction. The court's role in enforcing private agreements does <u>not</u> formally transform such private law as contracts and other commercial law into public law. This commercial law empowerment of private parties to make private law, which governs their transactions and which can be enforced in the courts, promotes commercial and entrepreneurial behavior, highly valued activities in our capitalist economic system.

The theory of public law, exemplified in the model of criminal law, is that the sovereign, either federal or state, is a party to the action. For example, criminal actions are prosecuted by public prosecutors who act in the name of the state in enforcing the penal code rules prohibiting murder, larceny, etc. against all residents in the state or nation (state or federal penal code). Other examples of public law include state and federal constitutions and administrative law (e.g., a social security hearing or a public assistance "fair hearing" in which a public official, the Commissioner of the Federal Social Security Administration or the Commissioner of the State Department of Social Services, is a party to the proceeding).

Do you appreciate how the involvement of the federal or state sovereign as a party in a proceeding against a private party triggers a panoply of basic procedural protections (e.g., in a criminal law action that threatens liberty, the Fourth, Fifth and Sixth Amendments to the federal Constitution)?

CHAPTER

FOUR

INTRODUCTION

McBoyle is a case in criminal law which is an example of public law. It is the state against the defendant. In most first-year courses, however, it is not public law cases that you'll be studying. Rather, it is private law cases like *Port Huron* (civil, not criminal, cases) that you'll be scrutinizing in torts, contracts, property, civil procedure, etc. In these subjects, it is typically two individuals, a plaintiff and a defendant, who are the parties to the lawsuit. The state is <u>not</u> a party. The plaintiff, who initiates the lawsuit, claims that the defendant, by action or failure to act, has violated a legal right of the plaintiff, and hence, the plaintiff has suffered damages. For these damages, resulting from the defendant's violation, the plaintiff claims a remedy, usually money.

Using the six-step process and applying the guidelines detailed in Chapter Two, please brief the following case in negligence (torts).

****

NEIL SAUER, an Infant, by ANN SAUER, His Guardian ad Litem, et al., Respondents, v. HEBREW INSTITUTE OF LONG ISLAND, INC., Appellant.

First Department, November 27, 1962.

* * *

APPEAL from a judgment of the Supreme Court, in favor of plaintiffs, entered April 6,1962 in Bronx County, upon a decision of the court at a Trial Term (CHARLES A. LORETO, J.), without a jury.

Carl J. Silverstein of counsel *(Turetzky & Cohen,* attorneys), for appellant.

Joseph R. Apfel for respondents.

BERGAN, J. The infant plaintiff, a camper at defendant's Summer camp, was injured while playing a game supervised by defendant's personnel. The infant was 13 years old and the game was a "water fight" between groups of campers of similar age, played on a grass-covered area in which opposing groups of boys doused each other with water from cups or water pistols.

In running away from an opponent, the infant plaintiff slipped on the grass and struck his head on a concrete walk at the side of the grass area. After a trial before the court without a jury, an award of $15,000 has been made to infant plaintiff and nominal damages to his father.

In our view of the record, this result is not warranted. The defendant, as the operator of a camp for boys, could not reasonably be made responsible in damages for the consequences of every possible hazard of play activity. It was required, rather, to guard against dangers which ought to have been foreseen in the exercise of reasonable care (*Klein v. Hoffman*, 15 A D 2d 899; *Weinstein v. Tunis Lake Props.*, 15 Misc 2d 432, affd. *sub nom. Derwin v. Tunis Lake Props.*, 9 A D 2d 9G0, motion for leave to appeal denied 10 A D 2d 711).

It has not been demonstrated that the water fight game was more hazardous than any ordinary camp activity involving running. It was inevitable in the game that the grass would become wet; and, indeed, in any such game among 13-year-old boys, that there would be tumbles and falls whether it was wet or dry.

To impose liability in this situation is to interdict the game itself, which in turn would so sterilize camping activity for boys as to render it sedentary. It would take a keen sense of the prescient to envisage that in running in the game the infant plaintiff would slip at the very point in the area where there was a concrete walk. Nor is it, indeed, clearly demonstrated that, in view of the infant plaintiff's bare feet, the wetness of the grass played any effective part in his falling.

The Trial Judge felt that the game itself "ha[d] every aspect of innocent play"; that the supervision was adequate and there was no "defect in the grounds on which the contest took place." (33 Misc 2d 785, 786.) He felt, however, that the game should have been played on sand and not on grass. This retrospective view of how the camp should have managed the game, upon which there can be reasonable difference of opinion, is insufficient to impose a liability on defendant, either as an evaluation of the facts of the case, or as a matter of law.

The judgment for plaintiffs should be reversed on the law and the facts and judgment entered for defendant, without costs.

RABIN, J. P., VALENTE, EAGER and STEUER, JJ., concur.

Judgment for plaintiff unanimously reversed, on the law and on the facts, without costs and the complaint dismissed, without costs. Settle order on notice.

****

Contrast your brief of *Sauer* with the brief detailed below.

AN EXCELLENT BEGINNER'S BRIEF

Sauer v. Hebrew Instit.
17 App. Div. 2nd 245
(1st Dept. 1962)

FACTS

This statement of key facts emerges from application of guidelines set forth on p. 16.

The appellate court used the trial court labels, the plaintiff and the defendant. The defendant was the appellant on appeal; the plaintiff was the respondent.

These elements of the c/a of tort negligence are not set forth in the opinion. They are obtainable from other cases, casebook, hornbook, professor's lecture. You cannot understand this case without knowing the elements of this cause-of-action.

P, 13-year old summer camper, participated in "water fight" between group of campers of similar age. "Water fight," supervised by employees of D-camp operator, played on grassy area; boys threw and shot water at each other. P ran, slipped on wet grass, "struck his head on concrete walk" next to grassy area and suffered injury.

P initiated c/a for tort neg. Elements: 1) existence of duty; 2) reasonable person standard of care; 3) breach; 4) causation (factual and legal); and 5) actual damages. Conflict centered on elements 2) and 3).

PROCEDURAL HISTORY

Brief procedural history provides legal orientation: who won what at trial; who was appealing.

P awarded $15,000 f/neg. tort (father: nominal damages) after trial without jury. D-camp operator appeals.

ISSUE

One-sentence issue-specification in question form. It incorporates some key facts, refers to applicable rule and pinpoints elements of rule at issue.

Is the D-camp operator liable in negligent tort for breaching its duty "to guard against dangers" which "ought to have been foreseen in exercising reasonable care when a 13-year old camper runs, slips and hurts his head on concrete during a supervised "water fight"?

HOLDING

Statement of holding: an answer to issue, incorporating some key facts meshed together with reference to applicable rule and pinpointing of elements of rule at issue. This is the law of the case.

No. The D-camp operator is not liable in negligent tort for breaching its duty to guard against dangers it ought to have foreseen in exercising reasonable care when a 13-year old camper runs, falls and is hurt on concrete while participating in a supervised "water fight."

JUDGMENT

Judgment is the result or disposition of the case.

Judgment of trial court for P reversed by appellate court.

This presentation of the court's reasoning identifies and categorizes the two major types of argument. By so doing, this presentation reflects apparent student understanding of the court's reasoning. The first argument concentrated on tying together key facts in an argument that the water fight was "innocent play" without fault by the D.

The policy argument concentrated on the desirable purposes served by the court's holding. Summer camp activity for boys can have a certain roughness. A contrary holding might bar such games and make such camping "sedentary."

Do you understand how the two arguments together provided an explanation and justification for the holding?

****

With the focus that comes from experience and confidence, at least the reasoning could be set forth more succinctly, as illustrated at right.

REASONING

First, factually, the ct. stressed that "tumbles and falls" are inevitable in "ordinary camp activity"; that the trial judge found that the water fight was "innocent play" with adequate supervision and no defect in grassy site of game. Trial judge's view that sandy area would have provided better game site was merely one retrospective opinion.

Second, the ct. stressed the policy implications of finding liability on these facts: it would "interdict the game itself" and "sterilize camping activity for boys" making it "sedentary." Who could foresee that the P would fall on this concrete walk? In essence, the ct. said that tort negligence does not—and should not—impose liability for harm from "every possible hazard of play activity"—only for those D ought to have foreseen in exercising reasonable care.

****

REASONING

Factual Argum.:

•"tumbles and falls" inevitable in "innocent play"
• no E of greater risk than in any camp running game
• no Mon. A.M. quarterbacking on site selection tr. judge

Policy Argum.:

Finding D liable here would:

• "interdict" water fights
• "sterilize camp act. f/boys." Risk here not foreseeable in exercising reas. care

****

A POOR BRIEF

Lacks case, date and citation.

Cryptic. Omissions include:
- *supervision*
- *concrete at the side of wet, grassy area where game occurred*
- *campers of similar age*
- *P was running*
- *elements of c/a for tort negligence*
- *elements of c/a apparently at issue*

The PROCEDURAL HISTORY step of the brief is omitted.

Far too broad a specification of issue. This is not the issue posed by these facts. This statement is a conclusory legal formulation which totally ignores the key facts.

An incorrect, broad issue-specification leads to an incorrect, broad statement of the holding. It provides <u>no</u> guidance to correct legal standard to be applied in deciding when liability should exist for which hazards.

The court's JUDGMENT, meaning the result or disposition, is omitted.

Not a reason. Rather, it is part of the correct holding (see p. 59.

Unnecessary to include string of citations.

FACTS

A young boy fell on concrete and hurt his head while engaged in a "water fight" with other campers. He received damages.

ISSUE

Is it reasonable to make the camp operator liable in tort negligence "for the consequences of every possible hazard of play activity"?

HOLDING

No. A camp operator is not liable in tort negligence "for the consequences of every possible hazard of play activity."

REASONING

The ct. stated that a camp operator is only required "to guard against dangers which ought to have been foreseen in the exercise of reasonable care. (*Klein v. Hoffman*, 15 AD2d 899; *Feinstein v. Tunis Lake Props.*, 15 Misc.2d 432, affd. *sub. nom. Derwin v. Tunis Lake Props.*, 9 AD2d 960, motion for leave to appeal denied 10 AD2d 711)."

This represents an effort to identify steps in the court's reasoning. It is also necessary, however, to categorize types of argument (e.g., factual, policy, persuasive authority) in order to understand the reasoning. Not all arguments are of equal legal status or of equal importance in a particular case.

The ct. also stressed the following:

• no demonstration that water fight was "more hazardous than any ordinary camp activity involving running."

• inevitable that in game "grass would become wet" and that "13-year-old boys" will tumble and fall "whether" grass "was wet or dry."

• "To impose liability in this situation is to interdict the game itself, which in turn would so sterilize camping activity for boys as to render it sedentary. It would take a keen sense of the prescient to envisage that in running in the game the infant plaintiff would slip at the very point in the area where there was a concrete walk."

• the trial judge said the game was "innocent play"; that the supervision was adequate and there was no "defect" in the grounds on which the contest took place.

Extensive quotations no substitute for identifying and understanding the particular types of argument.

• he felt, however, "that the game should have been played on sand and not on grass. This retrospective view of how the camp should have managed the game, upon which there can be reasonable difference of opinion, is insufficient to impose a liability on defendant, either as an evaluation of the facts of the case, or as a matter of law."

Perhaps you have noticed that the element most at issue here—a requirement "to guard against dangers which ought to have been foreseen in the exercise of reasonable care"—is quite abstract. You might ask yourself: which dangers ought to be foreseeable and what does reasonable care mean? Your initial reaction that various judges might easily decide differently the meaning of this element of the rule as applied to particular fact situations is borne out by the case that follows below.

You do know something, however, from this *Sauer* case. You know that the holding not only disposes of this case: it is also a precedent which must be applied by this court in future cases with **similar** facts and issues. That is a requirement of *stare decisis* which is central to our common law system. The holding is binding authority for this appellate court and for all inferior (subordinate) courts for future cases with similar facts and issues.

With this in mind, please brief the following case, also in the same appellate court as decided *Sauer*. Apply the steps and guidelines set forth in Chapter II. Your professor has asked you to **"reconcile"** the two cases—i.e., to explain the facts, issues, holdings and reasoning, as consistent (if you believe them to be so) or inconsistent (if you so believe). One hint: concentrate on exactly how the facts in the two cases are the same and exactly how they are different.

RICHARD GREAVES, an Infant, by His Mother and Natural Guardian, ADRIENNE GREAVES, et al., Respondents, v. BRONX Y.M.C.A., Appellant.

First Department, June 24, 1982

SUMMARY

APPEAL from a judgment of the Supreme Court in favor of plaintiffs, entered December 12, 1980, in Bronx County, upon a verdict rendered at a Trial Term (ALFRED J. CALLAHAN, J.).

***

APPEARANCES OF COUNSEL

Harvey J. Lippman of counsel *(Norman S. Goldsmith* and *Shari B. Rubin* with him on the brief; *Jones, Hirsch & Bull,* attorneys), for appellant.

Philip Hoffer of counsel *(Rose Hoffer, Frank J. Giordano* and *Harold Weisman* with him on the brief; *Frank J. Giordano, P. C.,* attorney), for respondents.

OPINION OF THE COURT

SANDLER, J.

Defendant appeals from a judgment for the infant plaintiff after a jury trial in an action for damages sustained when the plaintiff, then nine years old, was a camper at defendant's camp.

***

From the evidence presented by the plaintiff, the jury could reasonably have concluded that he sustained a severe injury to his elbow when he fell during the course of a game of ring-a-levio; that both campers and counselors participated in the game, the counselors as a separate team of "catchers"; that the game was played on a sloping grass area adjacent to a swimming pool; that the plaintiff slipped on a section of the grass that was damp as a result of water spilling over from the pool and the counselors having previously hosed the campers when they had emerged from the pool.

The principal issue presented on this appeal is the legal sufficiency of the evidence, the defendant contending that the case is controlled by the decision in *Sauer v Hebrew Inst. of Long Is.* (17 AD2d 245, affd 13 NY2d 913) in which, in a similar factual situation, a verdict in favor of the plaintiff was reversed, on the law and on the facts, and the complaint was dismissed.

As described in this court's decision in *Sauer* (*supra*), the plaintiff in that case, then 13 years old, was injured at a summer camp while playing a game supervised by the defendant's personnel. The game was a "water fight" between groups of campers of similar age, played on a grass-covered area in which opposing groups of boys doused each other with water from cups or water pistols. Running away from an opponent, the plaintiff in *Sauer* slipped on the grass and struck his head on a concrete walk on the side of the grass area.

In reversing a verdict after a nonjury trial in favor of the plaintiff, the court said (at p 246): "The defendant, as the operator of a camp for boys, could not reasonably be made responsible in damages for the consequences of every possible hazard of play activity. It was required, rather, to guard against dangers which ought to have been foreseen in the exercise of reasonable care".

Further on in the opinion, the following was said (p 246) "To impose liability in this situation is to interdict the game itself, which in turn would so sterilize camping activity for boys as to render it sedentary."

Recognizing the similarity of this case to the situation in *Sauer* (*supra*), we are not persuaded that *Sauer* is dispositive. The effect here of finding the evidence legally sufficient to support the jury's verdict would not be "to interdict the game itself". At issue here is not the appropriateness of the game that was played for the youngsters involved, but rather the judgment of the supervising counselors in selecting for the playing of the game a surface that might reasonably have been foreseen as adding needlessly to the risks inherent in the game itself.

It is appreciated that difficult problems of judgment may often confront counselors supervising the play activity of youngsters accustomed to strenuous physical exertions often accompanied by actions that involve some degree of risk. We appreciate the concern that a finding of liability in some camp situations may tend to "sterilize camping [activities] for boys as to render it sedentary." On the facts which the jury might reasonably have found in this case, however, we believe that a factual issue for jury determination was presented as to whether the playing of the game here on the described surface involved a foreseeable risk of unjustifiable danger. (See *Quinlan v Cecchini*, 41 NY2d 686, 689.)

Accordingly, the judgment of the Supreme Court, Bronx County (CALLAHAN, J.), entered on December 12, 1980, after a jury trial in favor of plaintiff for $90,000 should be affirmed.

Again, contrast your brief of *Greaves* with the following brief.

AN EXCELLENT BEGINNER'S BRIEF

Greaves v. Bronx YMCA
87 App. Div. 2nd 394
(1st Dept. 1982)

FACTS

This is a direct, fairly succinct statement of key facts. Again, the appellate court used the trial court labels, the plaintiff and the defendant. The defendant at trial was the appellant on appeal; the plaintiff at trial was the appellee on appeal.

P, 9-year-old summer camper, fell during a game of "ring-a-levio," and severely injured his elbow. Campers and counselors participated as separate teams. Game played "on a sloping grass area adjacent to a swimming pool." Grass wet. P initiated c/a f/tort neg. Elements: same as in *Sauer*, see p. 59. Again, conflict centers on elements 2) and 3), see p.59.

PROCEDURAL HISTORY

Brief, accurate statement of what happened at trial and who was appealing.

P won judgment for $90,000 for neg. tort after trial. D-camp operator appeals.

ISSUE

This formulation of the issue in question form incorporates key facts, reference to applicable rule, and pinpointing of elements of the rule at issue.

Whether the D-camp operator is liable in negligent tort for counselors' failing to foresee in exercising reasonable care that the selection of a sloping, wet, grassy area adjacent to a pool, on which the P fell and was injured which playing "ring-a-levio" "added needlessly to the risks inherent in the game itself"?

HOLDING

This is concrete statement of the law of the case: a reference to the general rule and elements of the rule, applied to particular facts of case.

Yes. The D-camp operator is liable in negligent tort for counselors' failing to foresee in exercising reasonable care that the selection of a sloping, wet, grassy area adjacent to a pool on which the P ran, fell and was injured while playing "ring-a-levio," "added needlessly to the risks inherent in the game itself."

JUDGMENT

The trial court judgment for plaintiff is affirmed

Judg. f/$90,000 affirmed.

The holding in Sauer is a controlling precedent for this case unless the court finds the instant facts to be distinguishable. It is imperative, therefore, to scrutinize **exactly** *how facts are similar and* **exactly** *how they are different.*

REASONING

• The ct. concentrates on distinguishing the facts of this case from the facts in *Sauer*. As related by the ct., the facts are **similar** in many ways:

Sauer	Greaves
summer camp	summer camp
water fight	ring-a-levio
P fell and was injured	P fell and was injured

Since fact patterns in different cases will always be different in some ways, the real question is which differences are sufficient to render the facts not similar and hence distinguishable.

The related facts are also **different** in some ways:

Sauer	Greaves
13-year-old P	9-year-old P
counselors supervised game	counselors played in game
P fell on concrete	P fell on grass
no defect in wet, grassy site of game	wet, grassy site of game was **sloping** and next to pool

No exact formula, no calculus, exists for this legal determination. In essence, it is a matter of lawyerly experience, judgment, and argument. While both game sites were wet and grassy, the site selected here was sloping and close to a pool. Using these facts to distinguish the facts in Sauer is an exercise in judgment and argument, not an ex cathedra pronouncement from Zeus on Mount Olympus.

Of all these differences, the ct. weighted the particular facts that the supervising counselors selected this **sloping,** wet, grassy area next to the pool as presenting a question for the jury: did this selection add needlessly to the inherent risks of the game?

Court agreed with the policy purposes presented in Sauer and argued that its holding here was fully consistent with such policy purposes.

• In an analysis of the policy purposes presented in *Sauer*, the ct. agreed that such games should not be "interdict[ed]" so as to "sterilize camping" activities and render them "sedentary." Ct. argued, however, that it was not doing this but only evaluating the judgment of the counselors in selecting a dangerous site for the game to be played.

If you happen to find the court's basis for distinguishing the facts in *Sauer* from the facts here in *Greaves* less than fully persuasive, you are in good company. A dissenter in the appellate court case, Justice Bloom, joined by Presiding Justice Murphy, also disagreed.

Please brief this dissent. In briefing a dissent, you should ordinarily be more succinct than in briefing the court's opinion. You should analyze a dissent to determine exactly how its marshalling of the facts, its formulation of the issue, its proposed holding and its reasoning **contrast** with comparable elements in the court's opinion, i.e., the opinion of the majority.

****

BLOOM, J. (dissenting). In August, 1976, plaintiff, then nine years of age, was enrolled in a summer day camp operated by defendant. On the day in question, plaintiff, and the others participating in the day camp, were at the Castle Hill Beach Club. In the late afternoon the campers emerged from the club pool. Their evening activity was to go to a Yankee baseball game. As they exited from the pool they were hosed down in accordance with the usual custom. They then dressed and had a typical camp supper consisting of hot dogs and hamburgers grilled at a barbecue pit. Since there was time to spare before they proceeded to the Yankee Stadium the campers and counselors engaged in a game of "ring-a-levio". The team of chasers consisted of three or four counselors while the team of those chased consisted of campers.

As the chase proceeded, plaintiff, who was dressed in jeans, a shirt, socks and sneakers, fell and injured his arm. He was taken to a hospital where it was ascertained that his elbow was broken. The arm was placed in a cast and plaintiff remained in the hospital for five days. Within three months the arm had healed and since that time plaintiff has actively engaged in athletics.

Thereafter this action was brought. It is bottomed on the claim that the "ring-a-levio" chase took place in an area surrounding the pool and that the defendant was negligent in permitting the game to be played in the vicinity of the pool. Plaintiff's fall, it is contended, resulted from the chase, during which he slipped on wet or damp grass. The jury returned a verdict in favor of the plaintiff in the sum of $250,000, and allocated 60% of the negligence to defendant and 40% to the infant plaintiff.

***

We are of the opinion that this case is governed by our holding in *Sauer v Hebrew Inst. of Long Is.* (17 AD2d 245, affd 13 NY2d 913). Accordingly, we would reverse and dismiss the complaint. In *Sauer* the plaintiff was a camper at defendant's summer camp. The campers were engaged in a game of "waterfight" in which the contending teams sought to douse their adversaries with water from cups or water pistols. Plaintiff, in an endeavor to avoid being sprayed with water, ran from an opponent. In so doing he slipped on the wet grass and struck his head on a concrete area immediately adjacent to the wet grassy area on which he slipped. In exonerating the defendant from liability we noted (p 246):

"The defendant, as the operator of a camp for boys, could not reasonably be made responsible in damages for the consequences of every possible hazard of play

- 67 -

activity. It was required, rather, to guard against dangers which ought to have been foreseen in the exercise of reasonable care ***

"It has not been demonstrated that the water fight game was more hazardous than any ordinary camp activity involving running. It was inevitable in the game that the grass would become wet; and, indeed, in any such game among 13-year-old boys, that there would be tumbles and falls whether it was wet or dry.

"To impose liability in this situation is to interdict the game itself, which in turn would so sterilize camp activity for boys as to render it sedentary."

* * *

The falls and tumbles of a nine year old at play are an inherent risk of any physical, competitive game. Only by forbidding the game can the risk be guarded against. However, to interdict such games is to make children's camping activities little more than a "baby-sitting" operation. Much as the law devotes itself to the protection of children it is powerless to protect them against childhood itself.

FEIN and ASCH, JJ. , concur in the opinion of SANDLER, J.;

* * *

MURPHY, P. J., and BLOOM, J., dissent in an opinion by BLOOM, J

Judgment, Supreme Court, Bronx County, entered on December 12, 1980, affirmed.

AN EXCELLENT BEGINNER'S BRIEF OF THE DISSENT

What the dissent illustrates is that legal reasoning is not mechanistic. Marshalling facts and arguments isn't simply identifying and categorizing them, it's also **weighting** *them—i.e., deciding which facts and arguments deserve to have more importance than others.*

The dissenters obviously believed that the key facts were that the P participated in a rough-house game of "ring-a-levio" in which, as in any running game, "falls and tumbles" were inevitable. The fact of the sloping , wet, grassy site of the game was not weighted as important and it was not seen as the source of the harm.

But what is the source of this weighting of different facts? I suggest it is in deeply held and contrasting gender attitudes about the need for risk-filled camping activities for boys.

[Note the power of this simple sentence. It is outstanding legal writing.]

Note the dissenter's policy concern that the majority's finding of liability "is to interdict the game itself," which threatens to "so sterilize camp activity for boys as to render it sedentary." These contrasting gender attitudes emerge from the life experience of the all-male judges, are clearly non-legal, and arguably the true ground of the decision, though never explicitly acknowledged of discussed.

Factually, the dissent did not single out the counselors' judgment in selecting the sloping,, wet, grassy area next to the pool as presenting added, foreseeable dangers to those inherent in playing games. Instead, it referred, in cursory and mostly conclusory language, to P's claim that the "ring-a-levio" chase took place "in an area surrounding the pool and that D was negligent in permitting the game to be played in the vicinity of the pool" where P slipped on wet grass.

The dissenters clearly believed that the harm to P came from the dangers **inherent** in the game itself, not from the selected site. Such a fall a P suffered is "an inherent" risk of any physical, competitive running game. Only by forbidding the game can the risk be guarded against. In an eloquent sentence, the dissenters summed up their view:

> Much as the law devotes itself to the protection of children, it is powerless to protect them from childhood itself.

The dissenters did not, therefore, find the facts of *Sauer* to be distinguishable. Thus, the holding of *Sauer* controlled. Given their weighting of the facts, their conclusion follows that the D camp-operator did not breach his duty "to guard against dangers which ought to have been foreseen in the exercise of reasonable care."

FUNCTIONS OF THE COURT EXEMPLIFIED IN *SAUER* AND IN *GREAVES*

Reviewing Application of Judge-Made Rules at Trial

In *Port Huron* in Chapter III, the Supreme Court of Iowa decided a claim of error committed by the trial court arising from the application at trial of a certain judge-made rule of contract to that fact situation. Here in *Sauer* and *Greaves*, the Appellate Division (First Department) of the New York State Supreme Court (which is the intermediate appellate court in New York State) decided a claim of legal error committed by the trial court arising from the application at trial of a certain judge-made rule of tort negligence to the fact situations embodied in *Sauer* and in *Greaves*. As in *Port Huron*, there is not a single reference in *Sauer* and in *Greaves* to any statute. This reflects the common-law truth that rules of tort negligence are substantially rooted in cases and in resulting case law. Court decisions in tort negligence cases usually flow from analysis of prior tort cases, not from analysis of statutes.

More specifically, in *Sauer*, the Appellate Division (First Department) decided that the trial judge in *Sauer* committed legal error in deciding in favor of the plaintiff. Why? As stated previously, the facts introduced as evidence by the plaintiff did not establish a breach of the defendant's duty to guard against dangers it ought to have foreseen in the exercise of reasonable care. Stated differently, the plaintiff did not meet its burden of proof (see p. 54) on these elements of reasonable care and breach.

In *Greaves*, however, the appellate court rejected the defendant's claim of legal error, deciding that the facts therein were sufficient to spell out a breach of the defendant's duty to guard against dangers it reasonably ought to have foreseen. Implicitly, the court here was affirming that the plaintiff at trial did meet his burden of proof on these elements of reasonable care and breach.

Fact-finding

In making these decisions, the appellate court was not deciding what are called questions of fact: e.g., it was not deciding that the plaintiff's witnesses were more credible than the defendant's witnesses; it was not deciding the extent of the plaintiff's injury. All of that was decided by the fact-finder at trial. In *Sauer*, the trial judge acted as fact-finder because the case was tried without a jury. In *Greaves*, the jury acted as fact-finder (the traditional role of the jury). The appellate court did not substitute its finding of facts for that of the fact-finder. Instead, its review was of claims of legal error committed by the trial judge—i.e., the facts, as found by the fact-finder at trial, did not establish a **prima facie** case. As a beginner, the appellate court review of this claim of legal error may appear to you to present a factual question. It does not. The categorizing of issues as either legal or factual is itself a matter of legal determination. To avoid confusion, follow your professor's guidance and observe how judges categorize issues in opinions.

Stare decisis

In deciding *Greaves*, the appellate court is exemplifying its role in adhering to the fundamental doctrine of **stare decisis**. In its opinion, *stare decisis* is not explicitly discussed. It is presupposed. It underlies the dissenters' contention (see court's opinion, p. 64) that "the case is controlled by the decision in *Sauer*" and the dissenters' statement (see p. 67) that "[w]e are of the opinion that this case is governed by our holding in Sauer." **Stare decisis** is the trigger for the struggle over the facts: are they sufficiently similar to the facts in *Sauer*? If so, there is ordinarily no escape: the precedent in *Sauer* must apply. If they are distinguishable, the precedent of *Sauer* is not controlling.

Just as judges argue that a second case is controlled, or not controlled, by a prior case, you will argue in class that two or more cases are consistent or not consistent. This is called reconciling and synthesizing cases. Typically, you will be queried (cross-examined may be more accurate) on exactly how the facts in two or more cases are the same and different. In addition, you may then be asked about the legal significance of these similarities and differences. Do the similarities explain the court's similar or different formulation of the issue, its specification of the holding and its reasoning? After scrutinizing the judges' reasoning in *Greaves*, it should be clear to you how fundamental is the process of reconciling and synthesizing cases.

No Ad-Hoc Decision-Making

There is an underlying principle animating the courts in both *Sauer* and *Greaves*. Neither trial nor appellate courts may engage in **ad-hoc** decision-making, seeking to do the "right thing" in each case in disregard of applicable rules and principles. Instead, courts must decide the particular controversy presented to it by the fact situation **only** in light of a more general rule or principle which covers a group of like controversies. **Ad-hoc** decision-making is rejected in our system of law.

ISSUES NOT CONSIDERED AND DECIDED IN *SAUER* AND *GREAVES*

Once again, it may be clarifying to enumerate some of the many issues not considered and decided in *Sauer* and *Greaves* and to understand exactly why such issues were not considered and decided. These include the following:

ISSUE	WHY NOT CONSIDERED
Whether "water fights" and "ring-a-levio" were played in the past without mishap?	*Irrelevant to the issue of breach of duty on specific occasions at issue.*
Whether the rules of these games were fair?	*Irrelevant. Courts are not arbiters of the fairness of games.*
Whether the trial judges and jurors had played these games and therefore were competent to decide.	*Irrelevant. Their authority to decide comes not from their experience at the games but from their status as judges and jurors.*
Whether the campers could have played safer games than a "water fight" and "ring-a-levio"?	*Irrelevant. Courts do not engage in such speculation—such "what might have been."*
Whether general court rules should be pronounced guiding camp operators conducting games in the future.	*A court decides only the particular controversy presented to it. It does not usually engage in such precautionary guideline formulations, however useful it might be to do so. (Perhaps such guidelines are an issue for an executive licensing agency.)*
Whether the trial judge thoroughly investigated all the facts involved in these injuries.	*Wrong. A judge in our system of law is <u>not</u> an investigator. A court ordinarily decides **only** the facts and issues presented to it by the parties.*
Whether these non-profit, charitable defendants have funds to pay a judgment for damages?	*Irrelevant to the determination of liability and damages.*
Whether the trial judges are liberal or conservative in their views of tort negligence?	*Their sworn duty is to select and apply the applicable legal rules, not their personal views.*
Whether these defendant camp operators could claim a defense of freedom of religion?	*Irrelevant. The issue is not an exercise of religious freedom but rather whether or not their conduct complied with their tort duty.*

Whether the issue, holding and reasoning should apply to a summer camp for girls?	*Irrelevant. A court decides **only** the controversy presented to it.*
Whether there are sexist assumptions underlying the court's discussions in *Sauer* and *Greaves* of appropriate summer camp activities for boys?	*Yes, but what is the legal significance of that insight on the rights and duties of the plaintiffs and defendants in* Sauer *and* Greaves*?*

COMMENT ON LAWYER QUA COUNSELOR

Sauer and *Greaves* provide an opportunity for understanding the role of a lawyer, not only as an advocate for a party in a lawsuit, but also as a counselor. Suppose you represented a camp operator, "Happy Times Camp" in 1962. Your client, the owner, had heard of the *Sauer* case from friends who operated the camp in *Sauer*. Your client asked you, "does *Sauer* mean I can tell the counselors to relax—they don't have to worry about the sites they select for water fights and other games?" In your lawyerly role as counselor, you might well have urged the camp operator to continue to direct the counselors to exercise not reasonable care but all possible care, both in selecting sites and in supervising games. In giving such advice, your objective is not simply to win a future lawsuit, but to prevent injuries and lawsuits. Your client's interests, and the campers' interests, are best served if injuries and lawsuits are prevented. Such advice, which exceeds your client's legal obligation, serves moral and social interests which are promoted by the law. In addition, if your client later heard of the *Greaves* result in 1982, she would have been especially delighted that she had followed your advice. The role of a lawyer as counselor can be an honorable and socially constructive role.

ADDITIONAL DEFINITIONS

TORTS (tortious conduct)—The American Law Institute's *Restatement of the Law of Torts (Second)* defines tortious conduct broadly as:

> ...conduct whether of act or omission...of such a character as to subject the actor to liability under the principles of the law of torts.

Major categories of such tort liability are specified:

> "an act which is intended to cause an invasion of an interest legally protected against intentional invasion," meaning **intentional torts** such as assault and battery (A slaps B in the face), false imprisonment, trespass, conversion, libel and slander;

or

> "conduct which is negligent as creating an unreasonable risk of invasion of a legally protected interest," meaning **negligent tort** illustrated in *Sauer* and *Greaves*;

and

> "conduct which is carried on at the risk that the actor shall be subject to liability for harm caused thereby, although no such harm is intended and the harm cannot be prevented by any precautions or care which it is practicable to require," meaning **strict liability tort**— e.g., liability for harm resulting from an unforeseeable defect in the brakes of a car.

DUTY—The *Restatement of the Law of Torts (Second)* defines duty as denoting:

> the fact that the actor is required to conduct himself in a particular manner at the risk that if he does not do so he becomes subject to liability to another to whom that duty is owed for any injury sustained by such other, of which that actor's conduct is a legal cause.

In *Sauer* and *Greaves*, the plaintiffs contended that the defendant-camp operators breached a duty owed to the plaintiffs. This particular duty in conducting games is to guard against dangers which ought to be foreseeable in the exercise of reasonable care, a duty grounded in tort negligence. In *Sauer*, the appellate court held that no such breach did occur. In *Greaves*, the same appellate court held that such a breach did occur.

LIABILITY—While there are many possible meanings which must be particularized in each case, one simple definition is to be "bound or obligated in law…responsible; answerable." Somewhat elaborated, it means that a person (or entity) is legally responsible to another person (or entity) to account for a breach of duty, either by action or failure to act, which has caused a harm to such other person (or entity), and for which breach and harm the law gives a remedy (e.g., money damages). In both *Sauer* and *Greaves*, the trial courts imposed liability on the defendant-camp operators—viz, judgments for plaintiffs for money damages. In *Sauer*, that imposition of liability was reversed by the appellate court; in *Greaves* it was upheld. In *Port Huron* in Chapter III, the judgment at trial for the plaintiff-seller for money damages imposed liability on the defendant-buyer and was affirmed by the appellate court. In *McBoyle* in Chapter II, the judgment of conviction at trial imposed criminal liability for the federal crime of interstate transportation of a stolen vehicle knowing it to be stolen, but the judgment of conviction was overturned by the Supreme Court.

INFANT and GUARDIAN AD LITEM—An infant is a person who has not yet reached the age of legal capacity or competence, sometimes called legal majority. At common law, twenty-one years was the dividing line; today, in most states, it is eighteen years. Please recognize, however, that this general rule has many particular exceptions from state to state. For example, driving licenses may be obtained at a younger age. Drinking alcoholic beverages in bars may not be legal until nineteen or twenty or twenty-one. In determining responsibility for crimes, the age varies; often it is sixteen but for some serious crimes (e.g., murder), sometimes younger.

In *Sauer* and *Greaves*, the plaintiffs were infants because they were nine and thirteen years old. They therefore lacked the legal capacity to initiate a lawsuit. Such a lawsuit is, therefore, typically initiated by a parent (or substitute) who is appointed a guardian ad litem. As stated by one court:

> A guardian ad litem is a special guardian appointed by the court to prosecute or defend, in behalf of an infant, a suit to which he is a party....Such a guardian is considered an officer of the court to represent the interests of the infant in the litigation.

POSTSCRIPT: NARROW VERSUS BROAD STATEMENTS OF HOLDING AND PRECEDENT

What you have learned so far are the basics of briefing and using cases for legal reasoning. In this postscript, I highlight a somewhat more advanced technique: narrower versus broader statements of a holding and the resulting precedent. The following four examples begin with a quite narrow statement of the *Greaves* holding and progressively broaden the statement of the *Greaves* holding by more general language. You'll recall the following statement of the holding in the excellent brief of *Greaves*:

> The D-camp operator is liable in negligent tort for counselors' failing to foresee in exercising reasonable care that the selection of a sloping, wet, grassy area adjacent to a pool on which P ran, fell and was injured while playing "ring-a-levio," "added needlessly to the risks inherent" in the game itself.

Please contrast this statement with the following, alternative statement of the holding in *Greaves*:

> The D-camp operator is liable in negligent tort for counselors' failing to foresee in exercising reasonable care that the selection of a site for the playing of a running game on which the P ran, fell and was injured, "added needlessly to the risks inherent" in the game itself.

Notice that the second statement of the holding is somewhat more general. Instead of the specific words "selection of a sloping, wet, grassy area adjacent to a pool," the latter statement refers more generally to "selection of a site." Instead of the specific words "playing ring-a-levio," the latter statement refers more generally to "playing of a running game." The effect of the more general language is to broaden the holding somewhat and hence to enlarge the scope of future cases to which this precedent **clearly** applies. For example, selection of a site with holes or selection of a site near a cliff or selection of a site for the playing of tag would manifestly be covered by the general language. This somewhat broader statement of the holding is also a perfectly proper specification of the *Greaves* holding. The prior statement of the holding is not wrong. It is simply a narrower or stricter statement (though some of your professors may regard it as too narrow).

Contrast the previous two statements of the holding with the following, alternative statement of the holding in *Greaves*. Concentrate on exactly how it is the same and how it is different.

> The D-camp operator is liable in negligent tort for injuries caused by supervisors' failing to foresee in exercising reasonable care that its supervisory efforts "added needlessly to the risks inherent" in camp activities.

Notice that this statement of the Greaves holding is substantially more abstract. Instead of "selections of a site" and "playing of a running game," you have the more general words "its supervisory efforts...." Instead of the words, "the P ran, fell and was injured," you have the more general words, "injuries caused by supervisors' failing...." While this statement of the *Greaves* holding is quite broad, your interest in arguing for the broader holding as the *Greaves* precedent would be appropriate if you represent a camper who was injured by lightning when the camp hiking director told the campers to take shelter under a lone tree during a lightning storm. A hike is not a game but it is surely "a camp activity" and the "supervisory efforts" of the hiking director clearly "added needlessly to the risks inherent" in a camp activity during a lightning storm.

Naturally, your adversary, the lawyer for the camp operator, would argue that this statement of the *Greaves* holding and precedent is erroneous because it is too broad: it goes far beyond the facts of *Greaves*. The *Greaves* holding and precedent, your adversary would argue, should be limited to the facts of *Greaves* and similar facts, i.e., selection of a site for a running game, not selection of a site for shelter during a lightning storm. You would respond: a) that these differences in facts do not distinguish the two cases because the facts are similar and it is not required that the facts be identical for *Greaves* to be controlling; and b) that this broader view of *Greaves* embodies its principle, what is sometimes called its **ratio decidendi** (see p. 52).

Who is correct? The trial judge who has to decide the new case provides the answer. The law authorizes a judicial decision-making procedure which results in a judgment for the plaintiff or for the defendant in the new case. If the issue is reviewed on appeal, the appellate judges will also decide by affirming or reversing the judgment of the trial court.

Lawyers and commentators (legal analysts) may disagree in law reviews or other articles or at meetings of bar association committees; they may even clearly have the more insightful analyses. Nevertheless, the decision of the court remains (until reversed or overruled). Why? The judges, not the lawyers and commentators, have the **power** to decide cases. The question is not which argument is correct in a philosophical, scientific or "objective" sense, but rather, which argument will be accepted and applied by a judge in a new case.

Consider, finally, this fourth statement of the *Greaves* holding and precedent:

> The D-camp operator is liable in negligent tort for injuries caused by its failing to foresee in exercising reasonable care that its actions "added needlessly to the risks inherent" in camp activities.

This is by far the broadest statement of the *Greaves* holding and precedent. Indeed, it is vulnerable precisely because it is too abstract, too sweeping, and so far removed from the key facts of *Greaves*: the counselors' selection of a sloping, wet, grassy site adjacent to a pool for the playing of "ring-a-levio" and a resulting injury. The first two statements of the *Greaves* holding and precedent are within the permissible spectrum of adversarial argument by lawyers and of judicial decision-making. The third statement is arguably within this spectrum. This fourth and final statement, however, is beyond the usual spectrum.

As this postscript demonstrates, there is considerable, but not unfettered, flexibility for argument and for decision-making in interpreting a holding and precedent. This postscript exemplifies additional functions of trial and appellate judges. A sophisticated understanding of using cases for legal reasoning requires an acquaintance with these functions, including the following.

TRIAL JUDGES' DISCRETION

Stare decisis

Trial judges exercise a substantial and inescapable discretion in deciding whether or not the facts and issues presented in a new case are similar to the facts and issues in a prior case cited as a precedent. There is no exact calculus or formula to apply in making this determination. Experience and lawyerly discretion are the guides. The application of the doctrine of *stare decisis* requires this exercise of discretion by the trial court. If the judge in exercising his discretion finds that the facts and issues are distinguishable (i.e., not similar), the precedent from the old case from the same or superior court is not controlling for the decision of the new case.

Extending and Limiting Precedent

If the trial judge in exercising his discretion finds, however, that the facts and issues in the old case from the same or superior court are similar to the new case, the doctrine of **stare decisis** requires that the precedent derived from the prior case be controlling. Nevertheless, the judge again exercises significant discretion in deciding exactly how to apply a judge-made rule contained in the holding of the prior case to the new case. In applying such a rule, a judge has the power to extend or limit the rule in applying it to the facts of the new case, and attorneys for both sides will be arguing for narrow versus broad, limiting versus extending interpretations. For example, the first, above-cited statement of the *Greaves* holding could then be **extended** in the ascending abstractions of the second and third statements of the *Greaves* holding. The judge in a new case could select one of the more general statements of the holdings even if the court in *Greaves* narrowly articulated the holding. The judge in a new case is not bound by a narrow statement of a prior holding or by a broad statement. In addition, in *Greaves* and in a good many other cases, the holding is not explicitly stated—it is implicit. This fact also encourages varying articulations by opposing lawyers, as well as by judges, of the case holding, of what the case "really stands for." With this insight into the power of judges to **extend** or **limit** a precedent, you can avoid a beginner's befuddlement because statements of a judge-made rule often vary somewhat from case to case. That variation is the expectation in the common law system, not an idiosyncratic deviation.

Choosing Between Two or More Applicable Rules

In addition to the above-explained exercises of discretion, a trial judge also has the power to decide which of two or more clearly or arguably applicable precedents presented by opposing lawyers should be applied to a new case. Contrary to what some beginners believe, there are many such cases. Again, experience and lawyerly discretion are the guides to such judicial decision-making, not any exact calculus.

Applying Statutory Rules

In applying statutory rules, trial judges also exercise substantial discretion. When the legislators enact statutory rules which include such abstract, broad-spectrum words as "reasonable," "equitable," "just," "appropriate," or "rules of reason," the legislature, in effect, invites judges to exercise a broad discretion in applying such rules so as to effect the policies intended by the legislators. When the legislators, in contrast, enact statutory rules which include more concrete, narrow-spectrum words, such as "transporting" a "motor vehicle" in "interstate commerce," "knowing it" to have been "stolen," the legislators are prescribing more detailed direction to trial judges who apply such statutory rules. As *McBoyle* shows, however, even apparently clear words such as "motor vehicle" can pose an issue when applied to a particular fact situation. In addition, just as trial judges must exercise discretion in the cases where two or more clearly or arguably applicable judge-made rules are presented by opposing lawyers, so too the trial judge must exercise similar discretion where two or more such statutory rules are presented.

Determining Meanings of Ambiguous Words

Trial judges must also exercise substantial discretion because facts, rules, precedents, principles and policies are expressed in words, and words are intrinsically a storehouse of ambiguity. Beware the one-word-one-meaning fallacy. Determining which one of the multiple meanings of a word is intended requires analysis of the word as part of a rule, precedent, principle or policy in light of the specific facts and issues in a particular case. *Sauer* and *Greaves* illustrate the ambiguity in the broad-spectrum word "reasonable." *McBoyle* illustrates the ambiguity in the apparently clear, narrow-spectrum word "motor vehicle." This intrinsic ambiguity of words helps to make the law dynamic, not static, to make it fun and a challenge, not boring.

APPELLATE JUDGES' DISCRETION

In addition to trial judges' discretion, appellate judges also exercise substantial and inescapable discretion in deciding appeals based on claims that trial judges have abused their discretion in determining whether or not facts and issues are distinguishable, whether precedent should be extended or limited, whether one judge-made or statutory rule should have been selected over another, whether rules with broad or narrow language have been correctly applied, and whether the meaning of words have been correctly determined. If the appellate judges are in the highest state appellate court, not the intermediate appellate court, their decision is usually conclusive. Judges in inferior courts, trial courts and any intermediate appellate courts are bound by the decision of the highest court in the jurisdiction on the legality of exercise of trial court discretion.

Slot Machines and Digestion

First-year students often react with dismay at the discovery that trial and appellate judges exercise substantial and inescapable discretion in applying and interpreting legal rules from cases and statutes. The dismay arises because of the shattering of a false image of judges as slot-machine automatons into whom facts are fed and out of whom spew rules and decisions. To the contrary, lawyers, legislators, trial and appellate judges make and remake the law in a living, ever-unfolding process. The law respects the past, but is not its prisoner. The law respects logic and precedent, but is more than a closed logical system locked into adherence to rigid precedent.

The shattering of the slot-machine automaton image of judges often leads to another equally misleading image: that judges do whatever they want to do; that their discretion is unfettered; that decisions depend exclusively on their digestion, love life, politics and prejudices. While there is some truth here and some bizarre judges exist, including bigots, psychotics, neurotics and egomaniacs, this image is an exaggeration.

What it overlooks is that institutional restraints also exist. Decisions of trial and intermediate appellate judges may be appealed. Most decisions of the highest appellate courts may also be changed by legislative action. Moreover, most judges are influenced by their legal training and by their experience as lawyers and judges to decide within a spectrum of acceptable reasoning and decision-making. In addition, most judges have a regard for their professional reputation among other judges, lawyers and commentators, and don't want to be reversed. Accordingly, most judges conscientiously strive to exercise their judicial discretion within legal boundaries.

What the beginning law student doesn't know is that those boundaries allow considerable flexibility for resourceful lawyers to argue and resourceful judges to decide. Judicial decision-making is like being on a cruise ship in the Atlantic. You can choose to go swimming in the pool, play ping-pong or snooze on the deck. The ship, itself, however, defines the boundaries of your choices, unless you decide to jump into the sea.

Discretion and Change

Do you see how this exercise of significant discretion by both trial and appellate judges allows gradual change in the law to accommodate the facts and claims urged by parties in new cases? The law incorporates respect for the river of cases from the past but it also allows judges a role in changing the law. The exercise of judicial discretion manifests the tension between the role of the law both in respecting the past and in accommodating the need to deal with new problems and evolving values. Understanding this creative tension in the law can help you to understand why rules and reasoning concerning the same issues may vary, especially over time. Rules and reasoning evolve as rules and reasoning are applied. Hence, this jurisprudential sounding point is quite practical: it sheds light on what is happening in the cases.

Contrasting power of the courts in *McBoyle* versus *Port Huron*, *Sauer*, *Greaves* and *Woods*.

In *McBoyle*, the power of the United States Supreme Court, absent any constitutional issue, is sharply fenced in. As mentioned, "the issue for the Court is determining congressional intent in enacting Section 2 of this statute, not what the Court thinks the meaning should be" (p. 30). This issue about congressional intent triggers the relevant repertoire of legal arguments traditionally applied in determining such legislative intent (pp. 26-27, 32, 33). The underlying reason why the Court is restricted to this particular repertoire of legal arguments flows from the principle of separation of powers. The Court has no power in *McBoyle* to substitute its own language and meaning, rather than the legislative meaning, in applying this statute. To do so would undermine democratic theory and majority decision making through the legislature.

In contrast, the power of the courts in *Port Huron*, *Sauer*, *Graves* and also *Woods*, in the next chapter, is quite different. No statutes are at issue. Instead, the rules at issue stem from cases, not statutes. The authority for these case-bound rules is the historic common law power of our courts to formulate, apply and interpret their own rules in traditional common law areas, including contracts (*Port Huron*) and torts.

Thus, the principle of separation of powers that underlies *McBoyle* is not dispositive, and the repertoire of legal arguments about determining legislative intent is irrelevant. Instead, a different repertoire of legal arguments is emphasized: precedent, the ordinary and exceptional meanings of ***stare decisis***, narrow versus broad statements of holding and precedent, the evolutionary character of the common law, etc.

Lastly, appreciating the different powers of the courts in interpreting statutes and interpreting their own case-based rules enables you to understand another difference that befuddles some law students. You now can clearly understand why courts in applying statutes stress the precise words of the legislature embodied in the statute (the expression of "the people's will"), while courts in applying common law rules often **vary** their own case-based rule language somewhat to fit the different factual and legal exigencies expressed from case to case.

CHAPTER

FIVE

INTRODUCTION

In *Sauer* and *Greaves* in the last chapter, lawyers and judges engaged in a routine, every day disagreement about the application of an undisputed, but somewhat vague element (the standard of reasonable care) of a legal rule of tort negligence, to a set of facts whose legal significance is quite disputable. Were the key facts that the playing of "ring-a-levio" on the sloping, wet, grassy area next to the pool created an added, unreasonable risk? Or were the key facts that this game had inherent risks against which tort law should not, and cannot, protect? To call the disagreement over these facts a "routine, every day disagreement" is not to slight its importance. The conflict was of pressing weight for the plaintiffs and defendants, for their attorneys, and, judging by the tone of the opinions, for the judges too.

In *Woods v. Lancet* (303 N.Y. 349 [1951]), discussed in this chapter, you will not see any conflict over which facts are key. Instead, the dispute is centered on whether an entrenched, common law (judge-made) rule of tort negligence should be affirmed or overturned. While appellate courts do not decide such issues every day, this type of case is a legal landmark and is the type frequently printed in casebooks used in law schools. Understanding the types of justification embodied in Judge Desmond's skillfully crafted opinion for the New York State Court of Appeals provides insight into the variety of types of reasoning typically employed in such landmark cases and in some other cases. In briefing *Woods*, apply the six-step approach with the guidelines and try especially to identify, categorize and **understand** the significance of these **types** of reasoning.

****

ROBERT C. WOODS, an Infant, by ESTELLE WOODS, His Guardian

ad Litem, Appellant, v.   JOSEPH LANCET, Respondent.

Argued October 4, 1951, decided December 6, 1951.

Woods v. Lancet, 278 App. Div. 913, reversed.

APPEAL from a judgment of the Appellate Division of the Supreme Court in the first judicial department, entered July 3, 1951, affirming, by a divided court, an order of the Supreme Court at Special Term (HAMMER, J.) in favor of defendant, entered in

Bronx County, granting a motion by defendant for a dismissal of the complaint for failure to state a cause of action.

* * *

DESMOND, J. The complaint served on behalf of this infant plaintiff alleges that, while the infant was in his mother's womb during the ninth month of her pregnancy, he sustained, through the negligence of defendant, such serious injuries that he came into this world permanently maimed and disabled. Defendant moved to dismiss the complaint as not stating a cause of action, thus taking the position that its allegations, though true, gave the infant no right to recover damages in the courts of New York. The Special Term granted the motion and dismissed the suit, citing *Drobner v. Peters* (232 N. Y. 220). In the Appellate Division one Justice voted for reversal with an opinion in which he described the obvious injustice of the rule, noted a decisional trend (in other States and Canada) toward giving relief in such cases, and suggested that since *Drobner v. Peters* (*supra*) was decided thirty years :ago by a divided vote, our court might well re-examine it.

The four Appellate Division Justices who voted to affirm the dismissal below, wrote no opinion except that one of them stated that, were the question an open one and were he not bound *by Drobner v. Peters* (*supra*), he would hold that "when a pregnant woman is injured through negligence and the child subsequently born suffers deformity or other injury as a result, recovery therefor may be allowed to the child, provided the causal relation between the negligence and the damage to the child be established by competent medical evidence." (278 App. Div. 913.) It will hardly be disputed that justice (not emotionalism or sentimentality) dictates the enforcement of such a cause of action. The trend in decisions of other courts, and the writings of learned commentators, in the period since *Drobner v. Peters* was handed down in 1921, is strongly toward making such a recovery possible. The precise question for us on this appeal is: shall we follow *Drobner v. Peters,* or shall we bring the common law of this State, on this question, into accord with justice? I think, as New York State's court of last resort, we should make the law conform to right.

Drobner v. Peters (*supra*), like the present case, dealt with the sufficiency of a complaint alleging prenatal injuries, tortiously inflicted on a nine-month foetus, viable at the time and actually born later. There is, therefore, no material distinction between that case and the one we are passing on now. However, *Drobner v. Peters* must be examined against a background of history and of the legal thought of its time and of the thirty years that have passed since it was handed down. Early British and American common law gives no definite answer to our question, so it is not profitable to go back farther than *Dietrich* v. *Northampton* (138 Mass. 14), decided in 1884, with an opinion by Justice HOLMES, and, apparently, the first American case. Actually that was a death case, since the five-month infant, prematurely born, survived for a few minutes after birth. The principal ground asserted by the Massachusetts Supreme Court (138 Mass., at p. 17) for a denial of recovery was that "the unborn child was a part of the mother at the time of the injury" and that "any damage to it which was not too remote to be recovered for at all was recoverable by her" (the mother). A few years later (1890), in Ireland, the Queen's Bench Division, in a very famous holding, refused to allow a suit to be brought on behalf of a child born deformed as the result of an accident in defendant's railway coach, two of the Justices taking the ground that the infant plaintiff was not *in esse* at the time of the wrong, and the other two regarding the suit as one on the contract of carriage with no duty of care owing by the carrier to the unborn infant whose presence was unknown to defendant (*Walker v. Great Northern Ry. of Ireland*, 28 L. R. Ir. 69). A similar complaint was dismissed for similar reasons, and the dismissal affirmed by the Appellate Division, Second Department, in *Nugent v. Brooklyn Heights R. R. Co.* (154 App. Div. 667, appeal dismissed 209 N.Y. 515). It is significant that the Appellate Division's opinion in the *Nugent* case (*supra*) indicates that, had it not been for the contract-of-carriage theory and its supposed consequences, the writer of the opinion would have favored recovery. Other strong support for just treatment of prenatal wrongs (of another kind) is found also in the 1893 opinion of .Justice HAIGHT (later of this court) in *Quinlen v. Welch* (69 Hun 584); however, on appeal, this court found it unnecessary to pass on the point (141 N.Y. 158). There were, in the early years of this century, rejections of such suits by other courts, with various fact situations involving before-birth traumas (see *Allaire v. St. Luke's Hosp.*, 184 Ill. 359; *Gorman v. Budlong*, 23 R.I. 169; *Stanford v. St. Louis-San Francisco Ry. Co.*, 214 Ala. 611; *Newman v. City of Detroit*, 281 Mich. 60; *Magnolia Coca Cola Bottling Co. v. Jordan*, 124 Tex. 347; *Buel v. United Rys. Co.*, 248 Mo. 126; *Lipps v. Milwaukee Elec. Ry.&Light Co.*, 164 Wis. 272) and, quite recently, Massachusetts has reaffirmed the *Dietrich* rule (*Bliss v. Passanesi*, 326 Mass. 461). The movement toward a more just treatment of such claims seems to have commenced with the able dissent in the *Allaire* case (*supra*), which urged that a child viable but *in utero,* if injured by tort, should, when born, be allowed to sue; and the movement took impetus from the Wisconsin court's statement in the *Lipps* opinion (*supra*), that it was restricting its holding (of nonrecovery) to a nonviable child. Thus, when *Drobner v. Peters* came to this court in 1921, there had been no decisions upholding such suits, although the two New York lower court rulings above cited (*Nugent* and *Quinlen* cases, *supra*), were favorable to the position taken by plaintiff here.

In *Drobner v. Peters* (*supra*), this court, finding no precedent for maintaining the suit, adopted the general theory of *Dietrich v. Northampton* (*supra*), taking into account, besides the lack of authority to support the suit, the practical difficulties of proof in such cases, and the theoretical lack of separate human existence of an infant *in utero*. It is not unfair to say that the basic reason for *Drobner v. Peters* was absence of precedent. However, since 1921, numerous and impressive affirmative precedents have been developed. In California (*Scott v. McPheeters*, 33 Cal. App.2d 629) the Court of Appeal allowed the suit—reliance was there put on a California statute but that statute was not directly in point, since it directed only that "a child conceived, but not yet born, is to be deemed an existing person, so far as may be necessary for its interests in the event of its subsequent birth." That California statute merely codified an accepted and ancient common-law rule (see *Stedfast v. Nicoll*, 3 Johns.Cas. 18, 23, 24) which, for some reason, has not, at least in our court, been applied to prepartum injuries tortiously inflicted. In 1949, the Ohio Supreme Court (*Williams v. Marion R. T., Inc.*, 152 Ohio St. 114, rule reaffirmed by the same court in *Jasinsky v. Potts*, 153 Ohio St. 529) and Minnesota's highest tribunal (*Verkennes v. Corniea*, 229 Minn. 365), and in 1951, the Court of Appeals of Maryland (*Damasiewicz v. Gorsuch*, _ Md._ , 79 A. 2d 550) and the Supreme Court of Georgia (*Tucker v. Carmichael*, 208 Ga. 201) upheld the right of an infant to bring an action like the one we are here examining, without statutory authorization. The Supreme

Court of Canada had announced the same rule back in 1933 (*Montreal Tramways v. Leveille*, [1933] 4 Dom. L. Rep. 337). In New Jersey a strong five-to-ten dissent (written by the Chief Justice) unsuccessfully urged the same view (*Stemmer v. Kline*, 128 N.J.L. 455) [1942]). In England there seems to be no controlling precedent (see Professor Winfield's comprehensive article in 4 U. of Toronto L. J. [1941-1942] 285 *et seq.*). Of law review articles on the precise question there is an ample supply (see 20 Minn. L. Rev. [Feb., 1936] 321-322; 34 Minn. L. Rev. [Dec., 1949] 65-66; 48 Mich. L. Rev. [Feb., 1950] 539-541; 35 Cornell L. Q. [Spring, 1950] 648-654; 1951 Wis. L. Rev. [May] 518-528; 50 Mich. L. Rev. [Nov., 1951] 166-167). They justify the statement in Prosser on Torts, at page 190, that: "All writers who have discussed the problem have joined in condemning the existing rule, in maintaining that the unborn child in the path of an automobile is as much a person in the street as the mother, and urging that recovery should be allowed upon proper proof."

What, then, stands in the way of a reversal here? Surely, as an original proposition, we would, today, be hard put to it to find a sound reason for the old rule. Following *Drobner v. Peters (supra)* would call for an affirmance but the chief basis for that holding (lack of precedent) no longer exists. And it is not a very strong reason, anyhow, in a case like this. Of course, rules of law on which men rely in their business dealings should not be changed in the middle of the game, but what has that to do with bringing to justice a tort-feasor who surely has no moral or other right to rely on a decision of the New York Court of Appeals? Negligence law is common law, and the common law has been molded and changed and brought up-to-date in many another case. Our court said, long ago, that it had not only the right, but the duty to re-examine a question where justice demands it (*Rumsey v, New York & N. E. R. R. Co.*, 133 N.Y. 79, 85, 86, and see *Klein v. Maravelas*, 219 N. Y. 383). That opinion notes that Chancellor KENT, more than a century ago, had stated that upwards of a thousand cases could then be pointed out in the English and American reports "'which had been overruled, doubted or limited in their application'", and that the great Chancellor had declared that decisions which seem contrary to reason "'ought to be examined without fear, and revised without reluctance, rather than to have the character of our law impaired, and the beauty and harmony of the system destroyed by the perpetuity of error.'" And Justice SUTHERLAND, writing for the Supreme Court in *Funk v. United States* (290 U. S. 371, 382), said that while legislative bodies have the power to change old rules of law, nevertheless, when they fail to act, it is the duty of the court to bring the law into accordance with present day standards of wisdom and justice rather than "with some outworn and antiquated rule of the past". No reason appears why there should not be the same approach when traditional common-law rules of negligence result in injustice (see *Hagopian v. Samuelson*, 236 App.Div. 491, 492, and see Justice STONE'S article on "The Common Law in the United States," 50 Harv. L. Rev. [1936], pp. 4-7).

The sum of the argument against plaintiff here is that there is no New York decision in which such a claim has been enforced. Winfield's answer to that (see U. of Toronto L. J. article, *supra*, p. 29) will serve: "if that were a valid objection, the common law would now be what it was in the Plantagenet period." And we can borrow from our British friends another mot: "When these ghosts of the past stand in the path of justice clanking their medieval chains the proper course for the judge is to pass through them undeterred." (Lord ATKIN in *United Australia, Ltd., v. Barclay's*

Bank, Ltd., [1941] A.C. 1, 29). We act in the finest common-law tradition when we adapt and alter decisional law to produce common-sense justice.

The same answer goes to the argument that the change we here propose should come from the legislature, not the courts. Legislative action there could, of course, be, but we abdicate our own function, in a field peculiarly nonstatutory, when we refuse to reconsider an old and unsatisfactory court-made rule. Perhaps, some kinds of changes in the common law could not safely be made without the kind of factual investigation which the Legislature and not the courts, is equipped for. Other proposed changes require elaborate research and consideration of a variety of possible remedies—such questions are peculiarly appropriate for Law Revision Commission scrutiny, and, in fact, the Law Revision Commission has made an elaborate examination of this very problem (1935 Report of N. Y. Law Revision Commission, pp. 449-476). That study was made at the instance of the late Chief Judge POUND of this court and was transmitted to the Legislature by the commission. Although made before the strong trend in favor of recovery had clearly manifested itself, the Law Revision Commission's comments were strongly in favor of the position taken in this opinion. The report, itself, contained no recommendations for legislation on the subject but that apparently was because the commission felt that it was for the courts to deal with this common-law question. At page 465, for instance, the report said: "The common law does not go on the theory that a case of first impression presents a problem of legislative as opposed to judicial power."

Two other reasons for dismissal (besides lack of precedent) are given in *Drobner v. Peters (supra)*. The first of those, discussed in many of the other writings on the subject herein cited, has to do with the supposed difficulty of proving or disproving that certain injuries befell the unborn child, or that they produced the defects discovered at birth, or later. Such difficulties there are, of course, and, indeed, it seems to be commonly accepted that only a blow of tremendous force will ordinarily injure a foetus, so carefully does nature insulate it. But such difficulty of proof or finding is not special to this particular kind of lawsuit (and it is beside the point, anyhow, in determining sufficiency of a pleading). Every day in all our trial courts (and before administrative tribunals, particularly the Workmen's Compensation Board), such issues are disposed of, and it is an inadmissible concept that uncertainty of proof can ever destroy a legal right. The questions of causation, reasonable certainty, etc., which will arise in these cases are no different, in kind, from the ones which have arisen in thousands of other negligence cases decided in this State, in the past.

The other objection to recovery here is the purely theoretical one that a foetus *in utero* has no existence of its own separate from that of its mother, that is, that it is not "a being *in esse*." We need not deal here with so large a subject. It is to be remembered that we are passing on the sufficiency of a complaint which alleges that this injury occurred during the ninth month of the mother's pregnancy, in other words, to a viable foetus, later born. Therefore, we confine our holding in this case to prepartum injuries to such viable children. Of course such a child, still in the womb is, in one sense, a part of its mother, but no one seems to claim that the mother, in her own name and for herself, could get damages for the injuries to her infant. To hold, as matter of law, that no viable foetus has any separate existence which the law will recognize is for the law to deny a simple and easily demonstrable fact. This child, when injured, was in fact, alive and capable of being delivered and of remaining alive, separate from its mother. "We agree with the dissenting Justice below that "To deny the infant relief in this case is not only a harsh result, but its effect is to do reverence to an outmoded, timeworn fiction not founded on fact and within common knowledge untrue and unjustified." (278 App.Div. 913, 914.)

The judgments should be reversed, and the motion denied, with costs in all courts.

* * * *

Contrast your brief of *Woods* with the excellent brief set forth below.

AN EXCELLENT BEGINNER'S BRIEF

FACTS

This statement of facts is as precise, succinct and conclusory as the court's statement of the facts. Note the severity of the claimed injuries.

Infant-P's complaint alleged that while viable in mother's womb in 9th month of mother's pregnancy, D negligently inflicted "such serious injuries" that upon birth the P was "permanently maimed and disabled."

In Woods, *an entire rule, rather than an element of a rule, or particular language, was at stake.*

P's c/a f/neg. tort against D barred by precedent from *Drobner v. Peters* (1921) in the same court: infant-P has no c/a f/neg. tort f/injuries neg. inflicted by D while infant was a viable foetus

.

PROCEDURAL HISTORY

While a clear understanding of the procedural situation is basic in briefing each case, here it was even more important in determining exact issue at stake: whether or not such infant-plaintiff should have a right to a cause-of-action and be authorized to prove his case at trial.

D's motion to dismiss P's complaint before trial as legally insufficient granted by trial court on ground that facts alleged in said complaint, even if all regarded as true, did not establish a recognized c/a. P had no rt. to a c/a based on authority of *Drobner v. Peters*. App. Div. affirmed, on judge dissenting. Case now in NYS Ct. of Appeals (highest appellate ct.).

ISSUE

For your purposes, you should specify more precisely than Judge Desmond's short-hand articulation of the issue (see p. 80). It was all right for the judge, but it is too broad for you.

Should the precedent established by *Drobner v. Peters* which denied a cause-of-action in tort for the D's negligent infliction of injuries when the infant-P was a viable foetus in its mother's womb, be overruled as inconsistent with justice?

HOLDING

It should be overruled: an infant has a cause-of-action in tort for the D's negligent infliction of injuries when the infant was a viable foetus in its mother's womb.

JUDGMENT

Judgment of the Appellate Division reversed (motion to dismiss P's complaint should be denied). (Case proceeds to trial, settlement, etc.).

REASONING

First, the ct. concluded there was "no material distinction" between facts of *Drobner v. Peters* and *Woods*.

(Hence, it wasn't possible to distinguish the two cases factually and thereby avoid application of precedent derived from *Drobner* holding. Applying **stare decisis**, this precedent ordinarily should be applied.)

Second, ct. surveyed the **legal thought** underlying the ***Drobner*** precedent. Key Mass. case in 1884 denied c/a: *Dietrich v. Northampton*. In *Drobner* in 1921, Ct. of Appeals adopted rule from *Dietrich*.

> *Drobner* ct's reasoning: no precedent (most important reason.)

Third, ct. contrasted lack of precedent prior to *Drobner* with "numerous & impressive affirmative precedents" after 1921 in many states and Canada.

An excellent formulation of the issue leads to an excellent formulation of the holding, which announced a new, common-law rule for this state.

P won the right to a cause-of-action in negligent tort and had to prove his case at trial.

Unlike Sauer *and* Greaves *in Chapter IV, the facts here in* Woods *were found by ct. to be "similar" to* Drobner. Drobner *was "on point."*

Student explicitly articulates what court opinion implied.

The court's survey of legal thought leading to the holding in Drobner *was not unimportant. It's clear objective was to lay a foundation for later rejection of the* Drobner *precedent.*

Of various reasons specified in Drobner *for its holding, the court stressed lack of precedent as most important. Note that this lack of precedent referred also to out-of-state cases and even to out-of-country cases. Such cases are persuasive, nonbinding authority on the New York Court of Appeals from the standpoint of stare decisis.*

Note the court's logic: if lack of authority was the chief reason for the Drobner *holding, that reason no longer existed. Why? "Numerous and impressive affirmative precedents" now existed. The* Drobner *precedent is analytically undermined by the removal of its main rationale.*

The commentators (law writers), especially the influential Prosser, are marshalled for additional support.

Also, many law review articles all agreed, e.g., Prosser: "all writers" condemned old rule & urged creation of a c/a here.

This conclusion is manifestly a culminating step in the court's argument so far.

Thus, "chief basis" for *Drobner* holding ("lack of precedent") no longer existed.

Ct. says in effect: stare decisis is fundamental but so is right & duty of highest state appellate court to change common law rule to accord with justice. Remember the interest at stake here: this infant "came into the world permanently maimed and disabled" by the defendant's negligence. This interest, (and other such future interests), provided a catalyst for the court's reasoning.

Fourth, ct. argued c.l. is dynamic, not static: ct has rt. and duty to mold, change & modernize c.l. rules to serve "justice."

In our governmental system of separation of powers, the legislature and the court both have the power to alter such a judge-made rule. Court need not await legislative action. Legislative advantage in holding hearings, in listening to experts testify, and in doing research, is not pertinent here. Why?

Fifth, ct. need not defer to remedial legis. action on "old" "unsatisfactory ct-made rule." Legis. & ct. both have power to change it. Moreover, NYS Law Rev. Comm. has studied issue and recommended new rule.

1) Change is a matter of moral principle here: a claim of justice, not of utility or of fact.

2) In any event, the Law Revision Commission has already investigated and recommended changes.

Alleged difficulties of proof present only routine difficulties handled every day.

Sixth, two other grounds for *Drobner* holding are rejected:

1) No merit in argument of difficulties of proof, which are not greater here than in other tort cases, espec. Workmen's Comp. cases.

Courts decide only what they must decide. Courts are loath to decide broad theoretical issues presenting sweeping political, philosophical or theological beliefs. Courts usually decide cases on narrowest ground presented by facts and issue of particular controversy.

2) Ct states that it is unnecessary to deal with "purely theoretical" issue that foetus is not "'being in esse.'" Facts, issue and holding in this case refer only to legal sufficiency of complaint alleging a c/a for neg. injury to a viable foetus later born alive.

Note here that the holding is expressly confined to a viable foetus later born alive. Note too, however, that viability would arguably cover a foetus less than nine months (e.g., a seven or eight-month old foetus).

****

****

REASONING

With experience and confidence, however, your statement of the reasoning might resemble this

• *Drobner v. Peters,* 1921 Ct. App. case which denies c/a here is "on point" but ct declines to follow it.

• *Drobner* holding based mostly on "lack of precedent."

• Since *Drobner* holding in 1921, num. and impress. precedents in States & Canada, & support from commentators.

• Hence, "lack of precedent" basis f/*Drobner* changed.

• Ct. has *power* & *duty* to change old c.l. rule to serve justice.

• No merit to other *Drobner* arguments of diff. of proof (like other T cases) and to theoret. issue re foetus a "being in esse" (not necess. to decide).

FUNCTIONS OF THE COURT EXEMPLIFIED IN *WOODS*

Stare Decisis and Justice

In *Woods,* you see a dramatic example of the highest court in a state, the New York State Court of Appeals, overruling an entrenched, thirty-year old rule of its own making and establishing a contrary rule for all New York State courts. The drama rises in what the Court of Appeals does not explicitly address: subordinating the ordinary, day-to-day meaning of the doctrine of *stare decisis.* The court itself states that the facts in *Woods* present "no material distinction" from the facts in *Drobner.* It is elementary then that the rule incorporated in the *Drobner* holding ordinarily should apply. The drama emerges, too, from the fundamental policy interests entangled with the *stare decisis* which might on the face of it seem to be sacrificed, including the following:

- our courts decide controversies according to a general rule, not on an ad hoc basis

- citizens may rely on established legal rules in ordering their business relations and in conducting their lives without fear that such rules will be "changed in the middle of the game"

- lawyers should be able to counsel those who seek their advice with reasonable certainty about established rules and with ability reasonably to predict which behavior will result in liability and which will not

In this skillfully crafted opinion, the court does not systematically discuss these matters. It does not, however, neglect them altogether. Against the argument of reliance on rules for ordering commerce (and social life), Judge Desmond's curt response is "…what has that to do with bringing to justice a tortfeasor who has no moral…right to rely on a decision of the" court? The judge here is referring to the fact that the defendant appears to be a clear tortfeasor as to the mother's injuries. Implicit in this response is also a rejection of the possible argument that the court's decision slights the lawyer's role in counseling clients about established rules and in predicting which behavior will and will not result in liability. How could a tortfeasor such as the defendant here be so counseled or his liability predicted? Undoubtedly, Judge Desmond would also reject the first argument as inappropriate: no *ad hoc* decision-making was implied in the *Woods* holding or reasoning. *Woods* is decided by a holding that will apply to like cases in the future.

Judge Desmond's opinion for the court persuasively illustrates that the fundamental doctrine of *stare decisis* does not mean that precedents must be slavishly followed. There are exceptions. As the opinion illustrates, there is excellent authority, indeed many precedents, for overruling old precedents "to bring the law into accordance with present day standards of wisdom and justice" (e.g., *Funk v. U.S.* 290 U.S. 371, 382). Following old precedents in new cases is not absolute. Hence with a more sophisticated understanding of *stare decisis*, the argued conflict between the doctrine of *stare decisis* and the *Woods* holding fades away.

Inherent in the court's claim of the justice to be served in *Woods* is the principle that evolving conceptions of justice should be served by an evolving common law. The court here subordinated the following of precedent to a claim of justice. It would be foolhardy, however, to assume that precedent will always defer to justice. Precedent will triumph in at least some cases against a claim of justice. In addition, claims of utility—of economic, social or political benefit for a majority or for a large number of people—will also occasionally triumph against old precedents. Our law serves many fundamental interests (or objectives) which courts must balance or rank in order of preference and subordination. Again, there is no simple formula or calculus for balancing or rank ordering.

Distinguishing Two Different Kinds of Appeals

In prior chapters, the appellate courts reviewed judgment of trial courts rendered after a trial. In *Woods*, the Court of Appeals reviewed a judgment of the intermediate appellate court which affirmed the judgment of the trial judge rendered without any trial. This trial court judgment was based on the pleadings of the parties, the complain of the plaintiff and the answer of the defendant. The trial judge, because of the *Drobner* precedent, granted the defendant's motion to dismiss the plaintiff's complaint because it did not allege a theretofore recognized cause-of-action for tort negligence. When the Court of Appeals overruled its *Drobner* precedent, it determined that the plaintiff's complaint did allege a recognized cause-of-action. This determination does not mean that a plaintiff automatically prevails. Not at all. The plaintiff must then proceed to try its case on the merits in the trial court. The plaintiff must establish the facts which spell out the elements of tort negligence. It is important for you to recognize the difference between an appeal based on claims of error after a trial of all the factual and legal issues, and an appeal, as in *Woods*, arising from a pre-trial granting of a motion to dismiss because of legal insufficiency of the plaintiff's pleadings, i.e., no recognized cause-of-action is alleged. In the latter situation, the plaintiff, if successful in the appellate court, must still prove his factual and legal allegations by a preponderance of the evidence in the trial court.

Woods thus illustrates also the significance in briefing of the procedural step: determining exactly what happened below and exactly who is appealing what claim of error. Figuring out the procedural status of the case helps you to unravel the meaning of the case—to look backward to see its origin and, hence, to understand the current issue, holding, judgment and reasoning.

Interacting of Substantive and Procedural Law

Woods also illustrates the interaction of substantive and procedural law. Substantive rules are ordinarily applied because of procedural triggers. For example, the trial court initially applied, as it must, the substantive rule embodied in the clear *Drobner* precedent and granted the defendant's procedural motion to dismiss the plaintiff's complaint because it did not state a then recognized cause-of-action. After the Court of Appeals overruled its old *Drobner* precedent, however, the trial court then applied, as it must, the new substantive rule embodied in the Court of Appeals' holding. Any subsequent procedural motion by the defendant to dismiss the plaintiff's cause-of-action would, of course, be denied because of the new precedent established by the Court of Appeals. The broadly applicable conclusion is that substantive rules are often applied in trial courts in response to procedural motions—e.g., a motion to dismiss the complaint, or a motion for a direct verdict (as in *Port Huron*, p. 78).

The Court In *Woods* Need Not Defer to the Legislature

Judge Desmond emphasized in the *Woods* opinion that both the state legislature and the Court of Appeals have the power to overturn the *Drobner* precedent. Since the *Drobner* precedent is judge-made, the Court of Appeals, as the highest appellate court in New York, need not defer here to the state legislature. Suppose for a moment, however, that the rule imposed by *Drobner* was imposed, instead, by a state statute. The Court of Appeals would then have **no power** to overturn the statutory rule. Why? Only the legislature which enacted the statute has the power to overturn it. With a statutory rule, the judicial power is to interpret and apply the rule, not to overturn it. In rare cases, the judicial power extends to invalidating a statute which is in conflict with a constitutional provision ("the fundamental law"). Contrary to what some beginning students believe, most courts rarely do so and for a most compelling reason: in a democratic system of government, a legislature's expression of the popular will should not lightly be disregarded.

Stare Decisis and *Res Judicata*

Even though the New York Court of Appeals in *Woods* in 1951 overruled its prior holding in *Drobner v. Peters*, the Court of Appeals did not reverse the judgment of *Drobner* rendered in 1921. That judgment survived the change of the rule and remained undisturbed. The reason is that the doctrine of *res judicata* applies (see p. 5) and bars retroactive invalidation of the judgment, even though the rule embodied in the *Drobner* holding was rejected by the Court in *Woods*. What is illustrated is that the doctrine of *res judicata* is applied quite strictly by the courts. Without this strict application, the policy served by the doctrine—promoting authoritative and final decision of controversies—would be undermined. In contrast, as *Woods* illustrates, the doctrine of *stare decisis* is more flexibly applied. In addition, in constitutional law cases, the application of the doctrine of *res judicata* is more complicated.

ISSUES NOT CONSIDERED AND DECIDED IN *WOODS*

Whether this claim of justice was well grounded in social theory and moral philosophy.	*Not necessary for the court's decision. Its power to entrench a claim of justice into judge-made law does not require that the claim be well recognized in social theory and moral philosophy. Law, social theory and philosophy are not identical.*
Whether this conclusory claim of justice should have been detailed.	*Not necessary to do so for simple reason that no judge on the court cared to dispute it.*

Whether the foetus here was a human being for all legal purposes.	*Irrelevant. Even a model illustration of what legal reasoning is **not**—a sweeping issue leading to a sweeping standard.*
Whether abortion is justified.	*Irrelevant. to the decision of this case.*
Whether the creation of the cause-of-action for the infant here was warranted on a cost-benefit analysis.	*Irrelevant. The right to a cause-of-action here was grounded on a claim of justice. Cost benefit analysis was not raised.*
Whether public opinion and the legislature approved of this decision and reasoning.	*Irrelevant. Judicial decision-making does **not** require majority, or even minority, support.*
Whether this family was affluent and therefore did not need money damages.	*Irrelevant. The cause-of-action is the plaintiff's, not the family's. In addition, there is no means test for the assertion of legal rights. A billionaire and an indigent both have the same formal right to a cause-of-action.*
Whether the mother here could have avoided this injury by taking another mode of transportation.	*Irrelevant. An accurate crystal ball is not a prerequisite to the assertion of a legal claim.*
Whether the defendant breached his legal duty owed to the plaintiff.	*Wrong. The Court of Appeals decided that the defendant owed the infant plaintiff a legal duty. The trial court must decide whether or not the defendant breached this duty, an element in establishing tort negligence.*
Whether the defendant's behavior caused (meaning both factual and legal cause) the plaintiff's injuries.	*Wrong. The trial court must decide this element of the plaintiff's cause-of-action for tort negligence.*
Whether the plaintiff was truly "permanently maimed and disabled" from the injury.	*Wrong. The trial court must decide this matter.*
Whether the display of the "permanently maimed and disabled" infant will influence the trial jury and prejudice the defendant.	*I hope it did. It is only unfair prejudice that may result in legal error. It is perfectly proper to prove the injuries by showing the baby at trial.*

If you can understand why these issues were not considered by the New York Court of Appeals in deciding *Woods*, you are gaining an awareness of the kinds of issues which are considered on appeal and the kinds of issues which are resolved in the trial court. Cultivating this awareness is essential for deciphering appellate cases and deepening your capacity to do legal reasoning.

A Few Final Definitions

Decisional law This is a synonym for case law ("common law") (see p. 3).

Cause-of-action. A cause-of-action is a legal claim recognized by the law of a jurisdiction (state or federal), alleging a harm resulting from a violation of a legal duty for which the law provides a remedy (e.g., money damages, specific enforcement of a contract, or an injunction commanding action or forbearance). In *Woods*, the cause-of-action was for negligent tort and the remedy sought was money damages.

Sufficiency of the Complaint In challenging the legal sufficiency of the complaint, a defendant claims that the complaint does not allege a cause-of-action, i.e., that the allegations of fact and law in the complaint do not constitute a recognized legal claim in a particular state or on the federal level. In a challenge to the legal sufficiency of a complaint, all the allegations of fact in the complaint are regarded as true. In deciding such a matter, a judge does **no** fact-finding. In *Woods*, the defendant moved to dismiss the plaintiff's complaint as insufficient on the basis that New York case law at that time provided "the infant no right to recover damages in the Courts of New York"—that, even conceding *arguendo*, that the plaintiff's assertion of facts was proved, no cause-of-action would exist because of the precedent established by *Drobner*.

VALUE OF PRECEDENTS

In addition to the overturning of a precedent by the highest appellate court in a jurisdiction, illustrated in *Woods*, courts and lawyers utilize a variety of arguments either to give added weight to a precedent or to detract from its significance.

First, certain courts, from time to time, enjoy special expertise and respect in specific areas and their opinions, therefore, may be viewed as carrying added significance. The opinions of the Second Circuit of the United States Court of Appeals concerning securities have received special attention. Many such cases emerge from the Wall Street financial community which is within the jurisdiction of the Second Circuit. The opinions of the United States Court of Appeals for the District of Columbia possessed added weight in the past in the area of administrative law. Some judges give added significance to opinions of state appellate courts which have enjoyed special prestige, including, for example, the New York Court of Appeals and the Supreme Court of California.

Second, sometimes you see references in cases to opinions by Holmes, Cardozo, Brandeis or Learned Hand. Some judges give opinions by such prestigious judges special attention.

Third, some opinions refer to a "unanimous" decision by a particular appellate court. Unanimous decisions carry at least a bit more weight.

Fourth, sometimes cases refer to a "frequently-cited" or "favorably-cited" or "frequently-followed" precedent. The implication is that the precedent is judicially popular and respected and should be applied by the court to which the argument is addressed.

Lastly, some court opinions buttress their application of a precedent by also arguing that the precedent accords with sound principle or policy or both.

Have you noticed that none of these arguments addresses the legal validity of the precedent. Indeed, validity is presumed and the arguments address only weight and respect. Such arguments are designed to persuade a trial or appellate court to apply a precedent in a specific case. Such arguments may be decisive in cases where two or more precedents are clearly or arguably applicable (see p. 5). As precedents multiply, there is a rise in the number of new cases to which two or more precedents are clearly or arguably applicable. Hence, the increasing importance of these various arguments aimed at weight and respect is clear. A variety of arguments are urged to detract from the weight or respect accorded a precedent.

First, if the prior case articulated the holding implicitly, it may be difficult to extract the clear holding. Opposing lawyers will probably argue for different formulations (see p. 20).

Second, if an appellate court agrees on the result, the judgment, but not on the holding and reasoning, precedent may be hard to determine. There may be several concurring opinions in which judges explain their views of the holdings and applicable reasoning and no single opinion may command majority support.

Third, a decision from an appellate court may be accorded less weight or respect if there was a dissent. Case references to a "sharply-divided court" or "a bare majority" manifest this weighting. The degree of negative weighting may depend on the reputation of the author of the dissent and its persuasive power. Some cases are distinguished by the illustrious quality of the dissent.

Fourth, some appellate opinions are categorized as "*per curiam*" opinions, i.e., opinions of the court without an acknowledged author. Such opinions are often summary, specifying a judgment but omitting the facts, issue, holding and reasoning. Hence, the precedential value of "*per curiam*" opinions is usually slight.

Fifth, lawyers commonly seek to restrict a precedent by limiting it to its facts. The argument is that the facts are so extraordinary or bizarre that the precedent should be limited to the extraordinary or bizarre facts of the case. Thus, the facts in the current case are always distinguishable. Opposing counsel is unlikely to agree with this factual characterization.

Sixth, appellate courts often multiply exceptions to a precedent before eventually overturning the precedent. The precedent endures despite the numerous exceptions, but its precedential weight is weakened.

These arguments are designed to persuade a court not to apply a particular precedent. Again, such arguments may be decisive if two or more clearly or arguably applicable rules are urged upon a court.

OPINIONS CAN BE FUN

If you believe judges to be devoid of wit, consider Justice Jackson's comments in *McGrath v. Kristensen*, 340 U.S. 162, 178 (1950). in which Jackson illustrates notable examples of reasons given by judges who declined to follow their own prior opinions.

> Baron Bramwell extricated himself...by saying 'The matter does not appear to me now as it appeared to me then.' *Andrews v. Styrap*, 2 L.T.R. (N.S.) 704, 706. And Mr. Justice Story, accounting for his contradiction of his own form opinion quite properly put the matter: 'My own error, however, can furnish no ground for its being adopted by this Court....' *United States v. Gooding*, 12 Wheat. 460, 478. Perhaps Dr. Johnson really went to the heart of the matter when he explained a blunder in his dictionary—'Ignorance, sir, ignorance.' But an escape less self-deprecating was taken by Lord Westbury, who, it is said, rebuffed a barrister's reliance upon an earlier opinion of his Lordship: 'I can only say that I am amazed that a man of my intelligence should have been guilty of giving such an opinion.'

CHAPTER

SIX

INTRODUCTION

In *Woods* in the last chapter, the controversy in the New York Court of Appeals pivots on whether a well-established common-law rule of tort negligence, created by the same Court of Appeals thirty years earlier, should be affirmed or overturned. In this chapter, in *State v. Shack*, 58 N.J. 297, 277 A.2d 369 (1971), the Supreme Court of New Jersey resolves a conflict of rights between a farmowner and migrant farmworkers who live and work on the farm. In resolving the conflict, the New Jersey Supreme Court considers, balances and rank orders a startling array of legal claims, including federal constitutional claims, factual and sociological claims, a congressional-intent claim, and a jurisprudential claim as to the real property interests protected by the state trespass statute.

Woods demonstrates how legal reasoning is dynamic, not static, and how legal reasoning is not simply technical, but also involves a philosophical/jurisprudential claim of justice. *Shack* demonstrates especially how legal reasoning can capture factual, sociological and moral reasoning as well as jurisprudential and constitutional reasoning. In addition, *Shack* vividly depicts how a new claim of legal right emerges from the vortex of political struggle within evolving historical contexts. Together, *Woods* and *Shack* dramatize that claims of right and legal reasoning can be much more than legal engineering. Technical craft is <u>always</u> inspired by jurisprudential perspective and historical context.

Shack also illustrates how a seemingly minor criminal violation, here a criminal trespass conviction, may sometimes explode with entangled legal claims into a landmark decision by the highest state court or even by the United States Supreme Court. *Shack* is, therefore, an example of a landmark real property case and is included in real property casebooks used in law schools. In briefing *Shack*, apply the six-step approach with the guidelines and strive to identify, categorize and understand these different legal claims and the diverse modes of reasoning applied by the Supreme Court of New Jersey.

****

State v. Shack

58 N.J. 297

State of New Jersey, Plaintiff-Respondent,

v.

Peter K. SHACK, and Frank Tejeras
Defendants-Appellants.

Supreme Court of New Jersey

Argued March 8 and 9, 1971

Decided May 11 1971.

Defendants, a field worker and an attorney for non-profit organizations formed to assist migratory farmworkers, were convicted of violating trespass statute in the Municipal Court of Deerfield Township and again on appeal in the Cumberland County Court, law Division, on a trial de novo, and they appealed. The Supreme Court, Weintraub, C.J., held that conduct of defendants in seeking to see farmworkers in privacy of their living quarters and without farmer-employer's supervision, was beyond reach of trespass statute.

Reversed and remanded with directions.

Max B. Rothman, Camden Regional Services, Inc., for appellants (David H. Dugan III, Peter K. Shack and Christian B. Peper, Jr. (of the Missouri bar), Camden Regional Legal Services, Inc., attorneys; on the brief).

Samuel J. Serata, Asst, Prosecutor, for respondent (Joseph Tuso, Cumberland County Prosecutor, attorney).

Barry H. Evenchick, Deputy Atty.Gen., for the Atty.Gen. of New Jersey, amicus curiae (George F. Kugler, Jr., Atty.Gen.).

Carl R. Lobel, Trenton, for New Jersey State Office of Legal Services, amicus curiae (Carl F. Bianchi, Trenton, attorney).

Frederick B. Lacey, U.S. Atty., submitted a brief on behalf of the United States, amicus curiae (Jerris Leonard, Asst.Atty. Gen., David L. Norman, Deputy Asst.Atty. Gen., and Joseph B. Scott, attorney, U.S. Dept. of Justice, of the D.C. bar, on the brief).

The Opinion of the Court was delivered by

WEINTRAUB, C.J.

Defendants entered upon private property to aid migrant farmworkers employed and housed there. Having refused to depart upon the demand of the owner, defendants were charged with violating N.J.S.A. 2A:170-31 which provides that "[a]ny person who trespasses on any lands * * after being forbidden so to trespass by the owner * * * is a disorderly person and shall be punished by a fine of not more than $50." Defendants were convicted in the Municipal Court of Deerfield Township and again on appeal in the County Court of Cumberland County on a trial *de novo*. R. 3 :28(a). We certified their further appeal before argument in the Appellate Division.

Before us, no one seeks to sustain these convictions. The complaints were prosecuted in the Municipal Court and in the County Court by counsel engaged by the complaining landowner, Tedesco. However Tedesco did not respond to this appeal, and the county prosecutor, while defending abstractly the constitutionality of the trespass statute, expressly disclaimed any position as to whether the statute reached the activity of these defendants.

Complainant, Tedesco, a farmer, employs migrant workers for his seasonal needs. As part of their compensation, these workers are housed at a camp on his property.

Defendant Tejeras is a field worker for the Farm Workers Division of the Southwest Citizens Organization for Poverty Elimination, known by the acronym SCOPE, a nonprofit corporation funded by the Office of Economic Opportunity pursuant to an act of Congress, 42 U.S.C.A. §§ 2861-2864. The role of SCOPE includes providing for the "health services of the migrant farm worker."

Defendant Shack is a staff attorney with the Farm Workers Division of Camden Regional Legal Services, Inc., known as "CRLS," also a nonprofit corporation funded by the Office of Economic Opportunity pursuant to an act of Congress, 42 U.S.C.A. § 2809(a)(3). The mission of CRLS includes legal advice and representation for these workers.

Differences had developed between Tedesco and these defendants prior to the events which led to the trespass charges now before us. Hence when defendant Tejeras wanted to go upon Tedesco's farm to find a migrant worker who needed medical aid for the removal of 28 sutures, he called upon defendant Shack for his help with respect to the legalities involved. Shack, too, had a mission to perform on Tedesco's farm; he wanted to discuss a legal problem with another migrant worker there employed and housed. Defendants arranged to go to the farm together. Shack carried literature to inform the migrant farmworkers of the assistance available to them under federal statutes, but no mention seems to have been made of that literature when Shack was later confronted by Tedesco.

Defendants entered upon Tedesco's property and as they neared the campsite where the farmworkers were housed, they were confronted by Tedesco who inquired of their purpose. Tejeras and Shack stated their missions. In response, Tedesco offered to find the injured worker, and as to the worker who needed legal advice, Tedesco also offered to locate the man but insisted that the consultation would have to take place in Tedesco's office and in his presence. Defendants declined, saying they had the right to see the men in the privacy of their living quarters and without Tedesco's supervision. Tedesco thereupon summoned a State Trooper who, however, refused to remove defendants except upon Tedesco's written complaint. Tedesco then executed the formal complaints charging violations of the trespass statute.

I.

The constitutionality of the trespass statute, as applied here, is challenged on several scores.

It is urged that the First Amendment rights of the defendants and of the migrant farmworkers were thereby offended. Reliance is placed on Marsh v. Alabama, 326 U.S. 501, 66 S.Ct. 276, 90 L.Ed. 265 (1946), where it was held that free speech was assured by the First Amendment in a company-owned town which was open to the public generally and was indistinguishable from any other town except for the fact that the title to the property was vested in a private corporation. Hence a Jehovah's Witness who distributed literature on a sidewalk within the town could not be held as a trespasser. Later, on the strength of that case, it was held that there was a First Amendment right to picket peacefully in a privately owned shopping center which was found to be the functional equivalent of the business district of the company-owned town in *Marsh*. Amalgamated Food Employees Union Local 590 v. Logan Valley Plaza, Inc., 391 U.S. 308, 88 S.Ct. 1601, 20 L Ed.2d 603 (1968). See, to the same effect, the earlier case of Schwartz-Torrance Investment Corp. v. Bakery and Confectionery Workers' Union, 61 Cal.2d 766, 40 Cal.Rptr. 233, 394 P.2d 921 (Sup.Ct.1964), cert. denied, 380 U.S. 906, 85 S.Ct. 888, 13 L.Ed 2d 794 (1964). Those cases rest upon the fact that the property was in fact opened to the general public. There may be some migrant camps with the attributes of the company town in *Marsh* and of course they would come within its holding. But there is nothing of that character in the case before us, and hence there would have to be an extension of *Marsh* to embrace the immediate situation.

Defendants also maintain that the application of the trespass statute to them is barred by the Supremacy Clause of the United States Constitution, Art. VI, cl. 2, and this on the premise that the application of the trespass statute would defeat the purpose of the federal statutes, under which SCOPE and CRLS are funded, to reach and aid the migrant farmworker. The brief of the United States, *amicus curiae,* supports that approach. Here defendants rely upon cases construing the National Labor Relations Act, 29 U.S.C.A. § 151 et seq., and holding that an employer may in some circumstances be guilty of an unfair labor practice in violation of that statute if the employer denies union organizers an opportunity to communicate with his employees at some suitable place upon the employer's premises. See NLRB v. Babcock and Wilcox Co., 351 U.S. 105, 76 S.Ct. 679, 100 L.Ed. 975 (1956), and annotation, 100 L.Ed. 984 (1956). The brief of New Jersey State Office of Legal Services, *amicus curiae*, asserts the workers' Sixth Amendment right to counsel in criminal matters is involved and suggests also that a right to counsel in civil matters is a "penumbra" right emanating from the whole Bill of Rights under the thinking of Griswold v. Connecticut, 381 U.S. 479, 85 S.Ct. 1678, 14 L.Ed.2d 510 (1965), or is a privilege of national citizenship protected by the privileges and immunities clause of the Fourteenth Amendment, or is a right "retained by the people" under the Ninth Amendment, citing a dictum in United Public Workers v. Mitchell, 330 U.S. 75 94, 67 S.Ct. 556, 91 L.Ed. 754, 770 (1947).

[1] These constitutional claims are not established by any definitive holding. We think it unnecessary to explore their validity. The reason is that we are satisfied that under our State law the ownership of real property does not include the right to bar access to governmental services available to migrant workers and hence there was no trespass within the meaning of the penal statute. The policy considerations which underlie that conclusion may be much the same as those which would be weighed with respect to one or more of the constitutional challenges, but a decision in nonconstitutional terms is more satisfactory, because the interests of migrant workers are more expansively served in that way than they would be if they had no more freedom than these constitutional concepts could be found to mandate if indeed they apply at all.

Property rights serve human values. They are recognized to that end, and are limited by it. Title to real property can not include dominion over the destiny of persons the owner permits to come upon the premises. Their well-being must remain the paramount concern of a system of law. Indeed the needs of the occupants may be so imperative and their strength so weak, that the law will deny the occupants the power to contract away what is deemed essential to their health, welfare, or dignity.

Here we are concerned with a highly disadvantaged segment of our society. We are told that every year farmworkers and their families numbering more than one million leave their home areas to fill the seasonal demand for farm labor in the United States. The Migratory Farm Labor Problem in the United States (1969 Report of Subcommittee on Migratory Labor of the United States Senate Committee on Labor and Public Welfare), p, 1. The migrant farmworkers come to New Jersey in substantial numbers. The report just cited places at 55,700 the number of man-months of such employment in our State in 1968 (p. 7). The numbers of workers so employed here in that year are estimated at 1,300 in April; 6,S00 in May; 9,800 in June; 10,600 in July; 12,100 in August; 9,600 in September; and 5,500 in October (p. 9).

The migrant farmworkers are a community within but apart from the local scene. They are rootless and isolated. Although the need for their labors is evident, they are unorganized and without economic or political power. It is their plight alone that summoned government to their aid. In response, Congress provided under Title III-B of the Economic Opportunity Act of 1964 (42 U.S.C.A. § 2701 et seq.) for "assistance for migrant and other seasonally employed farmworkers and their families." Section 2861 states "the purpose of this part is to assist migrant and seasonal farmworkers and their families to improve their living conditions and develop skills necessary for a productive and self-sufficient life in an increasingly complex and technological society." Section 2862(b) (1) provides for funding of programs "to meet the immediate needs of migrant and seasonal farm workers and their families, such as day care for children, education, health services, improved housing and sanitation (including the provision and maintenance of emergency and temporary housing and sanitation facilities), legal advice and representation, and consumer training and counseling." As we have said, SCOPE is engaged in a program funded under this section, and CRLS also pursues the objectives of this section although, we gather, it is funded under § 2809(a) (3), which is not limited in its concern to the migrant and other seasonally employed farmworkers and seeks "to further the cause of justice among persons living in poverty by mobilizing the assistance of lawyers and legal institutions and by providing legal advice, legal representation, counseling, education, and other appropriate services."

These ends would not be gained if the intended beneficiaries could be insulated from efforts to reach them. It is in this framework that we must decide whether the camp operator's rights in his lands may stand between the migrant workers and those who would aid them. The key to that aid is communication. Since the migrant workers are outside the mainstream of the communities in which they are housed and are unaware of their rights and opportunities and of the services available to them, they can be reached only by positive efforts tailored to that end. *The Report of Governor's Task Force on Migrant Farm Labor* (1968) noted that "One of the major problems related to seasonal farm labor is the lack of adequate direct information with regard to the availability of public services," and that "there is a dire need to provide the workers with basic educational and informational material in a language and style that can be readily understood by the migrant" (pp. 101-102). The report stressed the problem of access and deplored the notion that property rights may stand as a barrier, saying "In our judgment, 'no trespass' signs represent the last dying remnants of paternalistic behavior" (p. 63).

A man's right in his real property of course is not absolute. It was a maxim of the common law that one should so use his property as not to injure the rights of others. Broom, Legal Maxims (10th ed. Kersley 1939), p. 238; 39 Words and Phrases, "Sic Utere Tuo ut Alienum Non Laedas," p. 335. Although hardly a precise solvent of actual controversies, the maxim does express the inevitable proposition that rights are relative and there must be an accommodation when they meet. Hence it has long been true that necessity, private or public, may justify entry upon the lands of another. For a catalogue of such situations, see Prosser, Torts (3d ed. 1964), § 24, pp. 127-129; 6A American Law of Property (A. J. Casner ed 1954) § 28.10, p. 31; 52 Am.Jur., "Trespass," §§ 40-41, pp. 867-869. See also Restatement, Second, Torts (1965) §§ 197-2t l; Krauth v. Geller, 31 N.J. 270, 272-273, 157 A2d 129 (1960).

The subject is not static. As pointed out in 5 Powell, Real Property (Rohan 1970) § 745, pp. 493-494, while society will protect the owner in his permissible interests in land, yet

> "***[S]uch an owner must expect to find the absoluteness of his property rights curtailed by the organs of society, for the promotion of the best interests of others for whom these organs also operate as protective agencies. The necessity for such curtailments is greater in a modern industrialized and urbanized society than it was in the relatively simple American society of fifty, 100, or 200 years ago. The current balance between individualism and dominance of the social interest depends not only upon political and social ideologies, but also upon the physical and social facts of the time and place under discussion."

Professor Powell added in § 746, pp. 494-496:

> "As one looks back long the historic road traversed by the law of land in England and in America, one sees a change from the viewpoint that he who owns may do as he pleases with what he owns, to a position which hesitatingly embodies an ingredient of stewardship; which grudgingly, but steadily, broadens the recognized scope of social interests in the utilization of things.
>
> ***
>
> To one seeing history through the glasses of religion, these changes may seem to evidence increasing embodiments of the golden rule. To one thinking in terms of political and economic ideologies, they are likely to be labeled evidences of 'social enlightenment,' or of 'creeping socialism' or even of 'communistic infiltration,' according to the individual's assumed definitions and retained or acquired prejudices. With slight attention to words or labels time marches on toward new adjustments between individualism and the social interests."

This process involves not only the accommodation between the right of the owner and the interests of the general public in his use of his property, but involve also an accommodation between the right of the owner and the right of individuals who are parties with him in consensual transactions relating to the use of the property. Accordingly substantial alterations have been made as between a landlord and his tenant. See Reste Realty Corp. v. Cooper, 53 N.J. 444, 451-453, 251 A.2d 268 (19O9); Marini v. Ireland, 56 N.J. 130, 141-143, 265 A.2d 526 (1970).

The argument in this case understandably included the question whether the migrant worker should be deemed to be a tenant and thus entitled to the tenant's right to receive visitors, Williams v. Lubbering, 73 N.J.L 317, 319-320, 63 A. 90 (Sup.Ct. 1906), or whether his residence on the employer's property should be deemed to be merely incidental and in aid of his employment, and hence to involve no possessory interest in the realty. See Scottish Rite Co. v. Salkowitz, 119 N.J.L 558, 197 A. 43 (E. & A. 1938); New Jersey Midland Ry. Co. v. Van Syckle, 37 N.J.L 496, 506 (E. & A. 1874); Gray v. Reynolds, 67 N.J.L 169, 50 A. 670 (Sup.Ct.1901); McQuade v. Emmons, 38 N.J.L. 397 (Sup.Ct.1876); Morris Canal & Banking Co. v. Mitchell, 31 N.J.L. 99 (Sup.Ct.1864); Schuman v. Zurawell, 24 N.J.Misc. 180, 47 A.2d 560 (Cir. Ct.1946). These cases did not reach employment situations at all comparable with the one before us. Nor did they involve the question whether an employee who is not a tenant may have visitors notwithstanding the employer's prohibition. Rather they were concerned with whether notice must be given to end the employee's right to remain upon the premises, with whether the employer may remove the discharged employee without court order, and with the availability of a particular judicial remedy to achieve his removal by process. We of course are not concerned here with the right of a migrant worker to remain on the employer's property after the employment is ended.

We see no profit in trying to decide up on a conventional category and then forcing the present subject into it. That approach would be artificial and distorting. The quest is for a fair adjustment of the competing needs of the parties, in the light of the realities of the relationship between the migrant worker and the operator of the housing facility.

[2,3] Thus approaching the case, we find it unthinkable that the farmer-employer can assert a right to isolate the migrant worker in any respect significant for the worker's well-being. The farmer, of course, is entitled to pursue his farming activities without interference, and this defendants readily concede. But we see no legitimate need for a right in the farmer to deny the worker the opportunity for aid available from federal, State, or local services, or from recognized charitable groups seeking to assist him. Hence representatives of these agencies and organizations may enter upon the premises to seek out the worker at his living quarters. So, too, the migrant worker must be allowed to receive visitors there of his own choice, so long as there is no behavior hurtful to others, and members of the press may not be denied reasonable access to workers who do not object to seeing them.

It is not our purpose to open the employer's premises to the general public if in fact the employer himself has not done so. We do not say, for example, that solicitors or peddlers of all kinds may enter on their own; we may assume for the present that the employer may regulate their entry or bar them, at least if the employer's purpose is not to gain a commercial advantage for himself or if the regulation does not deprive the migrant worker of practical access to things he needs.

[4] And we are mindful of the employer's interest in his own and in his employees' security. Hence he may reasonably require a visitor to identify himself, and also to state his general purpose if the migrant worker has not already informed him that the visitor is expected. But the employer may not deny the worker his privacy or interfere with his opportunity to live with dignity and to enjoy associations customary among our citizens. These rights are too fundamental to be denied on the basis of an interest in real property and too fragile to be left to the unequal bargaining strength of the parties. See Henningsen v Bloomfield Motors, Inc, 37 N.J. 358, 403—101, 161 A.2d 69 (1960); Ellsworth Dobbs, Inc. v. Johnson; 50 N.J. 528, 555, 236 A.2d 843 (1967).

[5] It follows that defendants here invaded no possessory right of the farmer-employer. Their conduct was therefore beyond the reach of the trespass statute. The judgments are accordingly reversed and the matters remanded to the County Court with directions to enter judgments of acquittal.

For reversal and remandment: Chief Justice WEINTRAUB and Justices JACOBS, FRANCIS, PROCTOR, HALL and SCHETTINO—6

For affirmance: None.

****

AN EXCELLENT BEGINNER'S BRIEF

State v. Shack
58 N.J. 297, 277 A.2d 369 (1971)

FACTS

Key facts are extricated and pinpointed.

Two D's, Shack, a legal services lawyer, and Tejeras, a field worker for a migrant-aid program, enter P's farm—Shack to see one migrant worker re a legal case; and Tejeras to see another migrant worker re medical aid for removal of "28 sutures." P-farmer objected to Shack talking to migrants except in P's office and presence. D's declined and assert rt. to see migrants in "privacy of their living quarters." D's charged with crim. trespass upon refusal to depart.

PROCEDURAL HISTORY

Terse statement of mun. trial court disposition, initial appeal to County court, and present appeal to N.J. Sup. Court.

D's convicted of crim. trespass in Town Mun. court and again on appeal in County Court on a "trial de novo." N.J. Sup. court cert. D's further appeal to N.J.S. Court.

ISSUE

This formulation of the issue incorporates key facts and points to the rule utilized by the Court to decide the case.

Does a farmer have a possessory right, protected by a crim. trespass statute, to bar entry upon his farm to representatives providing "governmental services" to migrant workers living there?

HOLDING

This statement of the holding is a simple restatement of the issue in declarative form.

No. A farmer has no possessory right to bar reasonable entry upon his farm to representatives providing governmental services to migrant workers living there.

JUDGMENT

Student is aware of distinction between the holding and the judgment—the specific disposition of the criminal trespass conviction of the defendants.

D's Judgment of con. for crim. trespass reversed and D's are acquitted.

REASONING

Court's decision grounded in **policy** considerations:

Brief background factual and sociological analysis about plight of migrant farmworkers.

- Migrant workers are disad. segment of society: "rootless and isolated" and without economic or political power. Thousands come to N.J. during April-Oct. season.

Specification of federal anti-poverty legislation that funds legal, medical and other assistance to migrant workers.

- Fed. anti-poverty statute intended to aid migrant farmworkers with health, legal, ed., housing and other assistance employ D-lawyer and D-medical worker.

Court stresses that Congressional intent to aid migrant farmworkers could be defeated if farmers could simply bar entry to aiders as trespassers on the farms.

- Congress. intent defeated if migrant farmworker could be "isolated" from efforts to reach them. Key is commun.

Court illustrates its argument that prop. rts. are evolutionary and "not absolute" by reference to examples of historic common-law principle and limitations.

• "Prop. rts. serve human values."—not dominion over "destiny" of migrant workers, nor rt. to "isolate" workers from governmental programs aimed at aiding them.

Classic policy analysis supporting Court's view that legal meaning of ancient prop. rts. must be fine-tuned in light of modern facts, conditions and evolving conceptions of prop. and claims of society and of other individuals.

Rts. in real prop. are "not absolute" at C-L; e.g., no rt.. to use prop. to "injure others;" pub. and priv. necess. justifies entry upon real prop. (see Prosser). Prop. rts. are evolut. depending on mod. indus. and urban, pol. and social ideology and "phy. and social facts of time and place." Today: "ingred. of steward." is stronger—social interests.

Tenant's rt. to receive visitors is a traditional example of such a fine-tuning of landlord/tenant rts.

Thus, accomod. in prop. rts. between individ. owner and others connected with prop., e.g., tenant's rt. to receive visitors. Here, rts. of farmer and rts. of migrant farmworkers must be accommodated.

Court concludes first at a level of principle that a valid conception of prop. rts. does not include the rt. to bar governmental and private representatives seeking to aid migrant farmworkers.

Thus, Court concludes" farmer's rts. in real prop. include "no leg. need for a rt...to deny the worker the oppor. for aid available from fed., state or local services or "recogniz. charit. groups."

Court's broad principle is particularized to include facts of the instant case. Court's principle may also be articulated as a rt. of farmworkers.

Thus, reps. of such groups may enter to see workers at their "living quarters." "So too," mig. farmworker has rt. to receive privately visitors of "his own choice."

Student recognizes that Court, with lawyerly craft, carefully indicates its intention to limit the scope of its principle and holding by affirming traditional rts. of landowner.

Limitation: otherwise, farmer's rts. are clear to exclude others (e.g., peddlers and solic.) and reasonably to require visitors to identify themselves.

Terse indication that other defense claims to the court were not decided.

Other defense claims (1st and 6th Amend. and Suprem. Clause) are **not** decided.

FUNCTIONS OF THE COURT EXEMPLIFIED IN SHACK

Reconciling Conflicts in Rights

Shack illustrates an important slice of cases in which the court must resolve claims of conflicting rights. The farmer asserts a traditional right in our legal and popular culture—to determine who is authorized, and who is not authorized, to enter an owner's land, as well as the conditions of such entry. This claim of right resonates in our history, our consciousness and our folklore centered on the American dream: the ownership of property—the right to exercise dominion and control, whether of a vast or a tiny parcel, includes the right to determine entry. This right is a shared understanding in both a legal and popular sense.

The migrant farmworkers also have a right that resonates on another frequency—the legal and popular principle that our home is our castle, our refuge of repose, privacy and autonomy against the claims of the state and of others—applies to the "tempest-tost yearning to be free" as well as to the affluent. Our jurisprudence embodies this principle in valuing the privacy and autonomy of the migrant farmworker as much as that of the farmowner. Indeed, the principle should apply equally to those living in tents as to those living in castles. The conflict arises, however, because the migrant farmworkers who typically live on the farmer's land must exercise their rights in their living quarters which are part of the farmer's property. The types of claims urged upon the Court, and the modes of legal reasoning applied by the Court, illustrate part of the repertoire of claims and modes of legal reasoning that may validly be applied in solving such conflict of rights and in other cases.

Constitutional Claims

Initially, the New Jersey Supreme Court **excludes** a variety of federal constitutional claims urged upon the Court by the defendants, including First and Sixth Amendment claims as well as a claim that the Supremacy Clause bars application of the state trespass statute. In not deciding, indeed in choosing not even to explore formally these federal constitutional claims, the Court is narrowing its ground and scope of decision-making to state sovereignty—state court jurisdiction over interpretation of its state trespass statute and the nature of the property interests protected therein.

The general principles affirmed in this initial fencing in of what realms of law and issue(s) are decisive are a) that state courts, not federal courts, ordinarily are the **final arbiters** of the meaning of state statutes and of state common-law in the realm of real property; and b) that it is customary and a commendable exercise of the judicial virtue of economy for common law appellate courts to formulate and decide issues as *narrowly* as possible. The common-law tradition strongly discourages judicial exploration of issues not necessary to decide the specific case controversy presented for resolution. By defining which realms of law are at stake, state law rather than federal, the state court also ordinarily retains final control of the case, rather than heightening the risk of an appeal to the United States Supreme Court based on federal constitutional grounds.

Revealingly, the New Jersey Supreme Court explains its preference for "a decision in non-constitutional terms" as "more satisfactory" since "the interest of migrant workers are more expansively served in that way than they would be if they had no more freedom than these constitutional concepts could be found to mandate if indeed they apply at all" (*supra*, p. 96). The Court reveals its policy purpose to promote as far as possible the interests of migrant workers, and that state-law determination is a preferable legal basis for serving this end for two reasons: a) explicitly, that the federal constitutional claims "are not established by any definitive holding," and b) implicitly, that the nature of constitutional case law is ordinarily to establish only minimally required standards while non-constitutional case law is not comparably fenced in.

The reason for this restraint on federal constitutional case law is that the nationwide standards that may later be imposed by the United States Supreme Court are incorporated into our fundamental federal Charter of Liberties and may not be nullified or altered by any legislature, either federal or state, thereby insulating such rules from the arena of democratic politics and majority decision-making by a free people. Contrary to the belief of some first-year students, most federal courts, prompted by respect for the principle of federalism embodied in our system of dual federal and state sovereignty, as well as respect for the principles of separation of powers and majority rule, are reluctant to intrude with federal constitutional claims into such a traditional state common-law province as trespass and related real property rules.

A Jurisprudential Claim

The second type of legal reasoning applied by the Court is a jurisprudential claim—"Property rights serve human values"—and property rights are "not absolute" (*supra*, p. 97 and p. 98)—to frame in positive fashion the Court's Justification for its holding and judgment. The court argues for the validity of its broad jurisprudential claim by analogizing it to traditional common-law principles and examples of limitation of property rights, including the principle of public and private necessity that justifies entry upon property even against the will of the owner to save a transcending public value (e.g., fighting a raging brush fire justifies intrusion by the firefighters), or a transcending private necessity (e.g. freezing and lost hikers entering private land and breaking into a house to save their lives during a blizzard).

In addition to the use of historic common-law doctrines to justify its jurisprudential claim, the court applies another well-established type of reasoning: the closely related jurisprudential claim that the scope and nature of private property rights is "not static" but evolutionary and dynamic in response to the needs of "a modern industrialized and urbanized society . ...political and social ideologies...[and] the physical and social facts of the time and place under discussion" (*supra*, p. 98). Thus, the court embraces both use of historic common-law principles and an evolutionary view of the meaning of legal concepts of real property to support its broad jurisprudential claim that "property rights serve human values."

A Factual and Sociological Claim

The Court utilizes another type of legal reasoning—the use of factual and sociological analysis to pinpoint the importance of the interests posed by the seasonal presence within the state of thousands of migrant farmworkers who are "rootless and isolated...unorganized and without economic and political power" (*supra*, p. 97). Though framed mostly in factual and sociological language, the Court's use of this type of reasoning implicitly contains a moral claim—justice requires that the Court be responsive to the "plight" of the migrants (*Id.*). The Court's use of this factual-sociological-implicitly-moral form of reasoning is also a prelude to the following type of legal reasoning applied by the Court.

A congressional-intent claim

The "plight" of the migrant farmworkers led to legislation enacted by Congress in 1964 to aid these migrants and this explicit congressional purpose is applied by the New Jersey Supreme Court to re define in part the meaning of state trespass rules. After quoting from Congress' specification of the legislative purpose, including the provision of "health services" and "legal advice" to migrants, the Court concludes that "these ends would not be gained if the intended beneficiaries could be isolated from efforts to reach them." (*Id.*). While it is obviously not mandatory for the New Jersey Supreme Court to follow a specification of congressional intent in a federal statute in examining its state property rules, the highest court in New Jersey, nevertheless, clearly has the **power** to apply this congressional specification of purpose as a policy reason on the state level why migrants cannot be isolated on a farm under the legal pretext of the farmowner's right to control entry.

Narrow and broad views of a holding

Have you noticed that the New Jersey Supreme Court did not explicitly articulate its holding in *Shack*? You will look in vain for the magic word, "we hold," or equivalent words. With no explicit holding by the

-104-

Court, lawyers in new cases can easily argue for narrow or broad views of the true *Shack* holding and the resulting precedent. In fact, the Court aids and abets in this adversarial combat in new cases by providing ammunition to both sides.

For those lawyers (and judges) who desire to advocate a narrow view of *Shack* in a new case, the arguable holding is that the "defendants…invaded no possessory right of the farmer-employer" and "their conduct was therefore beyond the reach of the [New Jersey] trespass statute" (*supra*, p. 100). Is it clear to you how this narrow view of the holding tends to restrict the *Shack* precedent in a new case to the facts of *Shack*? The "defendants" refer to Shack, the lawyer, who entered upon the farm to see a migrant worker concerning a legal matter, and Tejeras, the field worker, who entered with Shack to see another worker concerning the removal of sutures. Their conduct in entering to see the migrant workers is characterized in **negative** and **limiting** language as "invad[ing] no possessory right of the farmer-employer" and therefore "beyond the reach of the trespass statute."

Contrast this narrow view with the use in a new case of a broad view of the *Shack* holding and the resulting precedent. This arguable holding is that "the migrant worker must be allowed to receive visitors [in his quarters] of his own choice, so long as there is no behavior hurtful to others" (*supra*, p. 99). Depending on the facts in the new case and the lawyer's adversarial needs, this broad view might alternatively be stated as "representatives of [anti-poverty] agencies and organizations may enter upon the premises to seek out the worker at his living quarters" (*Id.*). Contrast the negative, limiting language used in the narrow view in the prior paragraph with this more **expansive** language, especially "visitors [in his quarters] of his own choice" and "representatives…may enter…at his living quarters."

Shack illustrates again the insight that there is considerable, but not unfettered, flexibility for argument and for decision-making in interpreting a holding and precedent. While this is true in interpreting any prior case, the insight is of special importance where the court in the old case did not explicitly articulate its holding.

The principle of a case

The Court in its *Shack* opinion provides helpful language in arguing for a broad principle underlying the *Shack* holding. The "employer may not deny the worker his privacy or interfere with his opportunity to live with dignity and to enjoy associations customary among our citizens" (*supra*, p. 100). You might be wondering whether this specification of the *Shack* principle could also be presented as a broad view of the *Shack* holding? It could be so argued, especially if you, as a lawyer in a new case, felt that the trial or appellate judges might be receptive to such an argument. The articulation in the form of the *Shack* principle enables you to decouple the principle from the factual context and extend it to another factual context.

To illustrate, the *Shack* principle might be argued to gain access, for representatives of agencies that advocate for the elderly, to patients confined in nursing homes. As an advocate for the elderly, you would probably prefer to argue the applicability of the *Shack* principle to this quite different fact situation. By so doing, you are arguing that this principle can be decoupled from the *Shack* factual context, thereby enabling you to resist your adversary's stock response that *Shack* is irrelevant since the new facts are entirely different from the *Shack* facts (a patient is not a farmworker and the nursing home is not an employer of the patients). That stock argument has less force in arguing against the application of a principle than a holding. Holdings tend to be mired in the facts that birthed them and similar facts but principles are more peripatetic.

The interacting of historical context, politics and law

Historical Context and Politics

Shack also illustrates one form of interaction among historical context, democratic politics and law. The *Shack* holding and judgment would have been unlikely twenty or even ten years earlier. The manifest reason for this conclusion is that the federal statute relied on in *Shack* for its legislative purpose and designed to aid migrant workers became law in 1964, only seven years before the *Shack* opinion. That legislative enactment did not materialize without a social and political movement to aid migrant farm-workers. Indeed, the legislation is both a result of this movement and a spur to it. This legislation in 1964 and the related social and political movement are, in turn, closely related to a specific historical and political context after the assassination of President John Kennedy in 1963 and before the nation's immersion in the Vietnam War a few years later. From this super-charged era also emerged civil rights, anti-poverty, medicare, medicaid and federal aid-to-education legislation.

Politics Becomes Law

Once these social and political ideas are enacted into federal (and state) legislation, the ideas take on a new dimension: They are also law and enter into our legal culture. Thus, for example, the New Jersey Supreme Court is now authorized in its common-law decision-making to apply the specification of purpose from the federal migrant-aid statute as a legal policy reason for altering the meaning of the state concept of trespass. With this specification of purpose, the Court's use of it as policy is easily within the mainstream repertoire of legal argument. Without this specification of purpose, the Court's use of a migrant-aid policy purpose, while within the Court's power and entirely possible, is vulnerable to attack by some critics as a use of a political rather than a legal policy. Hence, the Court's opinion could be attacked as politically inspired, thereby possibly weakening its power as persuasive authority, a precedent and principle that may be adopted by state courts outside New Jersey. Within New Jersey, of course, the precedent is binding on all state courts.

Policy as a Bridge

Thus, policy provides one bridge between law and social and political movements within specific historical and political contexts. Some, not all, political and social policy is transformed into legal policy and rule, either by legislative enactment or directly by courts in exercising their common-law authority (see also, e.g., *Woods, supra* p.79-84).

Stated differently, basic new legal policy and rule come not from the banshees: They emerge from the struggle and experience of groups of people in a specific historical-political-social context. Thus, there is obviously no New Deal legislation (e.g., the Wagner Act and the Social Security Act) without a New Deal Administration and Congress; no environmental legislation without environmentalists; no feminist legislation without feminists; no civil-rights legislation without civil-rights advocates; no anti-abortion legislative and constitutional proposals without anti-abortion advocates; no capital punishment statutes without such advocates; and no massive, supply-side tax cuts in 1981 without supply-side advocates. The landmark case of *Brown v. Board of Education* in 1954, 347 U.S. 483, rejecting the separate-but-equal doctrine, would have been unlikely in 1896 when *Plessy v. Ferguson* established this doctrine; and *Plessy v. Ferguson*, 163 U.S. 537, would have been unlikely in 1954.

Law is more than politics

It is a *non sequitur*, however, to conclude that new legal policy and rule are reducible to their historical-political-social roots. That is an example of a simplistic reductionism. Aside from their roots, they are also legal policy and rule applied by courts (and executive agencies) with the conventional legal panoply, including constitutional framework, civil or criminal procedure, evidence, adversarial representation, decision by an impartial judge and jury, etc. Part of this legal panoply is a radically different rhetoric for formulating, analyzing and decision-making. The rhetoric of politics and social movements (e.g. "rightist," "leftist," "socialistic," etc.) gives way to the rhetoric of the law (e.g., policy, principle, rule, key facts, issue, hearsay, *prima-facie* case, preponderance of evidence, reasonable doubt).

The difference in rhetoric manifests the different, though not rigidly separate, layers of interconnected political and legal history, thought and decision-making. The legal realm is not simply derivative of the political, nor simply an elaborate epiphenomenon. Nor is it independent of history and struggle, a neutral body of value-free principles, a now waning claim more revealing of underlying jurisprudential and philosophical presuppositions than of the booming, bustling reality of the law-in-the-books and the law-in-action in the crucible of American experience.

Conclusion

While the particular use of these types of claims and modes of legal argument result in a holding and judgment in *Shack* in favor of the migrants and the defendants, there is nothing intrinsic in these claims and arguments that necessarily compels such a resolution of these conflicting rights.

ISSUES NOT CONSIDERED AND DECIDED IN *SHACK*

Whether the local legal services agency that employs Shack could operate an outreach sub-office in the living quarters of the farmworkers.	*Irrelevant to the instant facts, issue and holding.*
Whether the local migrant-aid agency that employs Tejeras could operate a medical outreach office in the living quarters of the farmworkers.	*Irrelevant to the instant facts, issue and holding.*
Whether an organizer for the United Farmworkers Union could enter and hold a public meeting in the living quarters of the farmworkers.	*Irrelevant to the instant facts, issue and holding.*
Whether an organizer for the United Farmworkers Union could enter and meet with interested farmworkers in their living quarters.	*Though not explicitly decided by Shack, such an entry and meeting would arguably fall within the right of a farmworker to "receive visitors there of his own choice."*

Whether the local fire persons may enter the plaintiff's farm against his will to fight a raging brush fire on a neighboring property.	*Authorized not by* Shack *but by the old common-law doctrine of public necessity.*
Whether a portion of the plaintiff's farm may be taken by the state with compensation for a widening of a public highway.	*Authorized not by* Shack *but by the old common-law and statutory doctrine of eminent domain.*

A FEW FINAL SUGGESTIONS ON BRIEFING

Q. Well, I've finished your chapters. Am I an expert now in briefing and understanding cases?

A. No. Not at all. You are a beginner, not an expert.

Q. What must I do to become more expert?

A. To be an advanced beginner, you must brief numerous cases, participate in class discussion, and gradually hone your skills in legal reasoning.

Q. Is there more to legal reasoning than what you have presented so far.

A. Lots more. This book presents an introduction to legal reasoning.

Q. What else should I read to learn more about legal reasoning?

A. It isn't reading alone that will light the path. It's performing. Nevertheless, with misgivings born of experience, I suggest the following readings. The danger in reading such *excellent* materials before you begin law school or in the first few weeks of it, is that you'll compound the natural beginner's confusion. Be careful. I recommend, therefore, that you look at some of the following materials after six or eight weeks of law school.

> *The Bramble Bush* by Karl Llewellyn
> *The Nature of the Judicial Process* by Judge Benjamin Cardozo
> *Case Analysis and Fundamentals of Legal Writing* by William Statsky and John Wernet

Q. Do you have any other recommendations?

A. Yes. Brief your assigned cases in the special notebooks with wide margins ("law ruled"). These notebooks are available in law book stores. You brief on the right. In the substantial left margin, you take notes in class as your professor discusses the case. What is your professor's analysis of the case? Why has she or he assigned the case? While many opinions discuss a number of issues, your professor may have assigned the case only to present one issue. This one issue may relate to substantive law or to an illustration of a lawyerly skill. The analysis of the case in class will reveal professorial priorities. Go with the current of your professor's pedagogic strategy. **Don't swim against the current.**

Save space in the notebook at the end of your brief. When you complete your brief before class, ask— what has this case added in light of the other cases you have studied in a specific segment of your professor's course? Don't assume that "added" refers only to knowledge of rules, principles and policies.

Instead, give equal weight as you reflect on the case to such knowledge and to demonstration of skills in legal analysis revealed by the case. Check and revise your brief after the class discussion of the case. Again, let your professor by your guide. Keep in mind that each case is best seen as a line in a chain of cases (see p. 11).

While most "shortcuts" turn out to be "longcuts," I also suggest that after a month or two of law school you should experiment with briefing at least some of your cases in the casebook. Yes, right in the casebook. You own it. You can write on the pages.

How do you do this? Take the more straightforward cases, ones in which the facts are intelligible; the procedural history is clear; the issue and holding are explicitly stated, are accurate and not cryptic; the reasoning is at least fairly well organized. Brief these cases by bracketing the relevant facts and underlining only the key facts. Write an **F** in the margin next to the cluster(s) of underlined key facts. Place a **P** next to the statement of the procedural history. Underline the explicitly stated issue and holding and place an **I** and **H** in the margin next to this underlining. Put a **J** next to the statement of the court's judgment, generally at the end of the opinion. With the reasoning, you number the arguments one by one, underline their most important parts and place an **R** in the margin. You should also strive to characterize each type of argument (e.g., policy; legal principle, etc.).

This briefing in the book works less well if the issue and holding are implicit and you must extract them and if the reasoning is confusingly presented and the facts are lengthy and rambling.

Experiment. Can you brief at least some of your cases in the case book? Do you learn as much as when you write out your brief in your notebook? Can you still respond well in class? Do you save substantial time? Generations of law students have briefed at least some of their cases in the casebook. You can too.

What do you do with the time you save? Review. Synthesize. Outline. Sharpen your skills in study groups. Practice answering the problems set forth in the old exams of your professors. I detail these and other methods in *How To Do Your Best On Law School Exams*.

A parting word which may encourage you through the thicket of the first year. While it is true that many core lawyerly skills are not taught by the case method of instruction in law school (see p. 13), it is nonsense that law school is unrelated to the real world of lawyering. The typical priority in the first year is legal reasoning which is a real-world priority. Whatever form your lawyering might assume—private practice, legal services, governmental work—your skill in legal reasoning is a *sine qua non*. You will use it every day. This cardinal truth is in no way diminished by the observation that varied other skills are also necessary.

CHAPTER SEVEN

A Jurisprudential Excursus

Modes of Legal Analysis*

*There is nothing more practical
than a good theory.*

Introduction

So far in this book, the presentation of this sequence of cases illustrates different types of mainly technical legal reasoning: in *McBoyle*, a variety of arguments to determine the meaning of the word, "vehicle," in a federal criminal statute as applied to an airplane; in *Port Huron*, a variety of arguments to determine the meaning of a common law rule of contract (a unilateral offer and acceptance) as applied to a particular fact situation; etc. From this presentation of cases, you might easily infer that learning the law is essentially a matter of learning a mass of technical rules and forms of legal reasoning to resolve issues arising from varied fact situations. The law then is at heart a technical reality that requires a legal engineering to decode it. Actually, this view is an encapsulation, a misleading reductionism, a tunnel-vision view of a multi-tunneled, a multi-dimensioned, reality.

In Karl Llewellyn's words:

> The major defect in [our] system [of precedents] is a mistaken idea which many lawyers have about it—to wit, the idea that the cases themselves and in themselves, plus the correct rules on how to handle cases, provide one single correct answer to a disputed issue of law. In fact the available correct answers are two, three or ten. The question is: Which of the available correct answers will the court select—and why? For since there is always more than one available answer, the court always has to select.
>
> "Remarks On The Theory of Appellate Decision And The Rules On Canons About How Statutes Are To Be Construed"
>
> 3 *Vanderbilt Law Review*, 395, 396 (1950)

One framework for selecting a "correct answer," and for justifying such selection, is jurisprudence. There are two dimensions to Llewellyn's question as applied to jurisprudence: the "which of the available correct answers..." is a factual inquiry about which of the available jurisprudential frameworks is to be utilized in answering; the "why" question inquires about justifying such choice. To **introduce** you to major jurisprudential perspectives, and their distinctive modes of formulating, analyzing and concluding, and the justification of such modes, I have convened a meeting of an imaginary fraternity of appellate judges, each of whom personifies a major jurisprudential outlook. I have asked each imaginary judge to review the cases presented in this book and to comment on which case(s) best illustrates her preferred jurisprudential viewpoint. While I have asked the judges to do their best to restrain their critical impulses, I recognize that it is humanly impossible for them to refrain from such comments concerning arguments and cases which they believe embody invalid jurisprudential choices.

The underlying premise is that every legal argument by a lawyer, every example of reasoning in a case, each case holding and judgment, exemplifies a jurisprudential choice. Many lawyers and judges are aware of these implicit and explicit jurisprudential choices. While many others are unaware, the implicit

---

* This chapter is inspired by Professor Lon L. Fuller's classic article, "The Case of the Speluncean Explorers," 62 *Harvard Law Review* 616 (1949).

jurisprudential choice is nevertheless there in **each** selection and application of an argument. Gradually becoming aware of these jurisprudential choices broadens and deepens your repertoire of arguments and enlarges your insight into the nature of law and the web that is our legal culture.

Judge Vigorous

I look at these cases dissected in Professor Delaney's book from my decades-long commitment to a carefully circumscribed judicial role within the framework of our political democracy. Our sworn duty as judges is to apply the existing written law, the will of the people, as enacted by our legislature and as developed by centuries of common law cases. In applying this body of existing law, our judicial duty is to be faithful to our constitutionally and jurisprudentially imposed role within this legal structure and culture.

We are faithful to our judicial role when we apply strict construction of these statutes and case holdings to resolve each controversy presented to us. We are not legislators elected by the people or free-wheeling angels of moral justice dispatched to right the wrongs of life. Our role in applying the strict, even literal, meaning of the statutory rules is to determine the objective propositional meaning intended, and actually embodied, in the statutory words, the output of legislative drafting, discussion, debate and vote; and the comparable objective meaning embodied in the case rules.

This is the meaning relied upon by the legislators and voters in the democratic process of enacting law, and it is the meaning that must therefore be applied by the courts in resolving the controversies presented in individual cases. Judicial respect for this objective meaning demonstrates respect for the distribution of powers that is central to our democratic theory and embodied in the constitutional principle of separation of powers: The legislature makes the statutory law in response to the will of the people but has no power to apply that law in individual cases. That individual application is the judicial power exercised by the courts.

If we embrace a broad view of our judicial role, the danger is that we intrude into, even usurp, the role of the legislature in making the law and into the role of the duly-elected executive, whether president, governor, mayor or town supervisor, in implementing governmental programs and in determining the executive realm of public policy. In a political democracy that truly respects the will of the people, the judicial role must be bridled and seek only the strict, objective meaning of the statutory and case rules rather than giving weight to what appeals to our subjective emotions of right and wrong. We are legal arbiters, not moral and social arbiters—that latter role is for others including legislators, mayors, governors, philosophers and moralists. In emphasizing this distinction, the intent is not to demean the importance of political and moral judgment, but only to stress the core truth that in principle law is separate from morality and politics. And judges apply law, not politics and morality.

It is therefore our sworn duty as judges to resist the ever present tendency to substitute our personal moral values for applicable legal rules in deciding cases where one party or the other would seem to capture our personal sense of right and wrong. Walking down that judicial path leads inescapably to **ad hoc** decision-making to do "justice" in the individual case at the expense of core values of democratic decision-making by the representatives of the people as well as core legal values of equal justice, certainty and predictability in the law.

I concede, of course, that I dislike enforcing both statutory and case rules that I oppose or that will result in a judgment for the "wrong" party from my political and moral point-of-view. But the old maxim that hard cases make bad law is certainly true and **ad hoc** decision-making surely offends the symmetry of the law and will wreak havoc upon other litigants in the future. In a democracy, the answer to bad law is political struggle to have the legislature change the law, and not for judges to usurp that legislative function and substitute their own subjective judgment for the democratic political combat of a free people. [Judge Freedom interrupts Judge Vigorous: We are all familiar with your jurisprudential perspective. I, for one, await your appraisal of Professor Delaney's selection of cases.]

Judge Vigorous continues:

I was just getting to those cases. Both the *McBoyle* and *Port Huron* cases (*supra*, pp. 26, 42) exemplify commendable judicial decision making and reasoning from my jurisprudential perspective. In *McBoyle*, the United States Court is acting in its limited but vital role as the final arbiter of the precise meaning of part of a federal criminal statute as applied to the unusual facts presented in a particular case. The issue is one of interpreting the intention of the Congress of the United States in enacting this criminal statute. In its judicial parsing of congressional intention, the Court utilizes classic sources of legislative intention, including congressional reports and debate and the meaning of the key word at issue, "vehicle", as used in other federal statutes and in state statutes. Even the Court's use of policy is well justified because the policies applied are well-established **legal policies** rather than the political or ideological policies often applied by Judge Freedom and her cohorts. I refer first to the core policy or principle that criminal statutes must give a clear and fair warning of which conduct is prohibited and of the penalty for violation. This principle is a virtual corollary of the bedrock principle of legality—no crime without [clear] law; no punishment without [clear] law.

Positivism serves democratic decision-making

Indeed, *McBoyle* illustrates how strict positivist reasoning and decision-making by appellate judges serves core legal principles of individual fairness (justice if you must), restraint of state power, separation of powers and majority decision-making by the legislature. In a historical era when statutes are proliferating, respect for democratic decision-making compels strict positivist reasoning and decision-making. Gone are the glory days when the King's common-law judges mostly made the law. Perhaps Judges Freedom and Pragmatic would prefer to have been judges in those halcyon days before political democracy triumphed with the emergence over centuries of an independent Parliament, the mother of our own Congress and state legislatures, a triumph of democracy forged in the blood of many political martyrs.

I also applaud the judicial restraint inherent in the Court's refusal in *McBoyle* to re-write the congressional statute either on "the speculation that, if the legislature had thought of it, very likely broader words would have been used," or on that hoary **post-hoc** fiction that the scope of the statute can be extended through a claim that the "policy" later found by the court to underlie the statute is served by such extension of meaning, a type of argument much favored by Judges Freedom, Pragmatic and Just.

Briefly, I also admire *Port Huron* which aptly illustrates strict appellate reasoning and decision-making in the common-law area of contracts. The Supreme Court of Iowa is reviewing an appeal of a defense claim that the trial court's direction of a verdict for the plaintiff was not supported by sufficient evidence. The trial court found that the undisputed facts established a unilateral contract, involving an offer that calls for performance and that can be accepted by performance of the act requested.

The trial court's reasoning is therefore an instance of strict **if-then** deductive reasoning—i.e., if the facts found by the trial court, here undisputed, fit within the category created by the applicable legal rule, then the rule applies and liability attaches. In reviewing the trial court decision and judgment, the reasoning of the Supreme Court of Iowa illustrates the use of traditionally appropriate legal-reasoning sources, including mandatory precedent from its prior decisions; persuasive authorities from the opinions of state courts outside Iowa; secondary authority such as *Corpus Juris* and the *American Law Reports*; and the writings of a distinguished commentator, Professor Williston.

I would like now to—[Judge Pragmatic interrupts: Thank you for your "succinct" presentation of your version of positivist jurisprudence. We will now hear from Judge Freedom].

Judge Freedom

> A statute merely declaring a rule, with no purpose or objective is nonsense.
> Karl Llewellyn

It is always a marvel to me that a person of Judge Vigorous' remarkable intelligence, education and experience can continue to embrace and apply such a truncated jurisprudential perspective. In the words of Judge Learned Hand:

> One of the surest indexes of a mature and developed jurisprudence is not to make a fortress out of the dictionary, but to remember that statutes always have some purpose or object to accomplish, whose sympathetic and imaginative discovery is the surest guide to their meaning.
>
> *Cabell v. Markham*, 148 F2d 737, 739 (C.C.A.2d 1945)

What Judge Vigorous overlooks is that the law, and thus the nature and scope of judicial decision-making, resonates on different frequencies. Statutes and case-based rules are not homogenous. They vary radically in their roots, nature and the policy purposes intended to be achieved by the legislature and by the appellate court which enacted and adopted them. Thus, the constitutional role of both trial and appellate courts in applying these rules to decide particular controversies must range at least as widely in nature, scope and purpose.

To begin with an affirmation of one of Judge Vigorous' arguments, I agree that a strict construction approach, a handmaiden of a narrowly circumscribed view of the judicial role, is well justified in interpreting criminal statutes as illustrated in *McBoyle*. Such a strict construction of criminal statutes promotes the fundamental policy purposes of liberty and autonomy by carefully fencing in the exercise of state power in criminal proceedings against individuals. Thus, one deep ground of strict construction of penal statutes is in the vital policy interests of liberty and autonomy that are thereby served. It is therefore the apex of tunnel vision, both in this illustration and generally, to separate the rule from its policy rationale.

Similarly, the rule of strict construction is also grounded in respect for the principles of majority decision-making by the legislature and of separation of powers (judges should not broaden the legislatively fixed scope of penal statutes by expansive interpretation). Nevertheless, this affirmation that strict construction of rules is sometimes justified, indeed required by governing policy purposes, actually supports my contention that courts must meticulously calibrate their powers in decision-making in accordance with the nature of the rules and policies they are called upon to apply to resolve particular types of controversy.

Strict construction and principles

But how does strict construction apply to trial and appellate decision making where the statutory and case rules to be applied sparkle with words indicating broad principles such as "equitable," "just," "fair," "reasonable," "proper," or "restraint of trade"? How are judges to determine the precise intention of the legislators in enacting rules that manifest such broad principles? The answer is unmistakably that judges must respond on a different frequency than strict construction. When legislators incorporate broad principles in statutes, they invite, indeed mandate, a broad view of the judicial role in applying such statutes to decide specific controversies. To apply a strict construction view to application of such principles is to reject the legislative mandate and thus to **breach our sworn constitutional duty to take care to faithfully enforce the laws.**

An understanding of the legislative process provides insight into the different nature of legislatively determined rules. Both federal and state legislators typically consider national or statewide problems presented to them, explore alternatives, and enact general legislation in response, either for the nation or for a specific state. Sometimes, their legislative responses to particular problems are specific (as in *McBoyle* where the criminal statute at issue prohibits the interstate transport of a stolen vehicle) and the implied legislative direction to the court, therefore, is to apply the canons of strict construction, to abide by severe restraint, to put on a tight-fitting judicial robe and role.

Indeed, there are many situations where the legislature has enacted very concrete rules, including, for example, the specification of statutes of limitation for various civil causes-of-action and criminal prosecutions, which must be initiated within two, three, five or more years; the specification of civil procedural rules requiring that various notices, answers to complaints, etc. be filed within twenty days, ninety days, or whatever period. The legislature has captured its intent in very concrete rules which can be straightforwardly applied. The meaning is fixed and easily discoverable in some of these concrete rules.

But even within the category of concrete rules, it is surely a distortion to articulate judicial interpretation as simply a task of determining "the objective propositional meaning intended, and actually embodied, in the statutory words…and in the cases" . This articulation presupposes that there is one objective meaning intended. In reality, however, different legislators and different judges may have intended different meanings, a reality that is complexified as judges today seek in good faith to determine "the objective propositional meaning" of old cases and statutes. With all respect to my distinguished colleague, the multi-dimensional challenge posed by interpretation even of many concrete rules is not aided by denying that there are difficulties, by resorting to obscuring fictions about what is at stake. The *McBoyle* decision convincingly illustrates this point (*supra,* p. 26). A simple, concrete statutory word, "vehicle," is capable of diverse meanings.

While many legal rules are concrete, many other rules are stated in more abstract words. *Their meaning is open-ended*, especially where the legislative response to a problem is that there is no legislative direction that can be reduced to a concrete rule that can be straightforwardly applied in each case. Thus, the legislature enacts **more abstract rules in the nature of principles or policy standards that authorize the judges to exercise far greater discretion** in deciding particular controversies, to wear, if you will, a looser-fitting judicial robe to match another mode of reasoning and fashion. To illustrate, in equitable distribution of property in divorce actions, the broad principle (standard) of equitable distribution of marital property to be applied in some states invites and authorizes the trial judges to exercise wide discretion in dividing marital property between the spouses. The breadth of the standard to be applied matches the wide scope of the different factual situations concerning marital property that are inherent in these divorce cases.

The centrality of purpose

In applying such wide discretion, the judges, both trial and appellate, must therefore incorporate the context and purpose(s) intended by the legislators in enacting such open-ended principles. In these cases, these purposes are central to specifying the meaning of such open-ended principles as "equitable," "just," "fair," "proper," etc. To illustrate, the principle of equitable distribution is designed to serve distinct policy purposes—that marriage is also an economic partnership and that ordinarily the distribution of marital property should be roughly equal. Even when the rules to be applied are more concrete, however, legislative purpose is relevant in specifying their meaning. For example, Justice 0. W. Holmes used such legislative purpose in *McBoyle* in deciding the precise meaning of "vehicle" in a federal criminal statute (see pp. 26-27). The conclusion is inescapable: policy is an irrepressible dimension in judicial interpreting/applying of legislative rules. Nor is this conclusion limited to statutory rules. While many case-based rules are concrete, many others are broad in the nature of principles—e.g., the "reasonable person," "proximate cause," the "best interests of the child," "shocking to the conscience," "unconscionability," "in the interests of justice," etc. With these broad common-law principles (though some of them can be statutorily embodied), policy is equally decisive in determining their meaning, though not legislative policy. The relevant policy flows from the common-law tradition of judge-made policy and is entrenched in case law.

Since this common-law tradition is demonstrably evolutionary, responding to new issues in light of evolving values and ever-changing social and historical context, the policy that drives these case rules derives not only from the past but also from the present and the unfolding future. Hence, judges, especially appellate judges, cannot "hide out" from their duty to determine which policies emerging from a contemporary era should be added to the common-law tradition by embodiment in appropriate cases. As judges, we are not prisoners of common-law history and its precedents derived from generations of dead judges. We should not be ruled from the grave. **We have a right, even a duty, to add those precedents and policies worthy of our era, its needs, and its values.**

Shack and the use of policy

From my jurisprudential perspective, therefore, the case that is most noteworthy in Professor Delaney's collection is *Shack* (*supra*, p. 94). The Supreme Court of New Jersey, under the inspired leadership of Chief Judge Weintraub, considered all the relevant legal claims, including constitutional arguments, congressional purpose(s) in enacting federal migrant-aid statutes, the plight of migrant farmworkers in our society, the moral idea that "property rights serve human values," and evolving "political and social ideologies . . . [and] physical and social facts of the time and place under discussion'" (*supra,* pp. 97-100).

Utilizing this "framework" of "policy considerations" (*Id.* at 100), the Court then interpreted the New Jersey trespass statute and relevant common-law property concepts to reach "an accommodation between the right of the owner [the farmowner] and the right of individuals who are parties with him...relating to the use of the property," [the migrants] (*Id.* at 99-100. *Shack* dramatically illustrates both the central importance of judicial use of "policy considerations," especially in cases where a conflict of rights is at stake and an array of rules, clearly technically relevant, are evaluated in light of decisive "policy considerations." Choice there muse be and the Supreme Court of New Jersey had the judicial courage to make that choice, thereby vindicating themes of justice that underpin our entire legal system and our culture.

I turn now to———[Judge Just interrupts: "Thank you Judge Freedom for your 'succinct' presentation. Time restraints require that..." Judge Vigorous then interrupts exclaiming in a loud voice: "I raise a point of personal privilege and demand time to respond to this political folly masquerading as jurisprudence." Reluctantly, after much murmuring and exasperated whispering among the judges, Judge Just gives Judge Vigorous two minutes for a rebuttal.]

Judge Vigorous' Rebuttal

In his presentation, Judge Freedom inadvertently exposes the jurisprudential bankruptcy of this policy mode of judicial formulation, analysis and decision-making. The opinion in *Shack*, the preferred model for Judge Freedom's promiscuous jurisprudence, is manifestly designed to manipulate a panoply of rules, principles and policies so that, in the Court's own words, "the interests of migrant workers are more expansively served..." This **unmistakable political objective** is the overriding policy among the many "policy considerations" that propels the Court's reasoning, holding and judgment.

All other policies, principles and rules are hostage to attaining this political objective. Even if one concedes, *arguendo*, that this political objective is also a legal policy, **the selection of this particular objective by the Court from among the array of available policy objectives is manifestly a political selection** to satisfy the subjective value choices of the judges. This opinion dramatically illustrates how policy-oriented jurisprudence authorizes judges to roam widely in the mountains and valleys of personal subjectivity, and then to cloak their subjective-value findings with the legal-sounding label of relevant policy that then drives the application of rules. This mode of formulating and analyzing is clearly a self-serving ideology for aggrandizing judicial power at the expense of the legislative and executive branches. Legislative rules become a text for decoding by judicially created interpretive schemes, a kind of self-serving literary license for wandering as far as some judges care to roam.

Policy undermines democratic decision-making

Though well-intended, your jurisprudential viewpoint undermines democracy by usurping political issues from the political arena of legislative and executive conflict and decision-making. Thus, though often masqueraded as a protector of human rights, the use of this mode of legal thinking erodes the principles of majority decision-making and of the separation of powers, thereby detracting from the rights of the people in favor of aristocratic decision-making by judges, who are appointed, not elected, and serve for life (federal judges), or who are elected or appointed and serve for long terms (many state judges). Over time, the incrementalizing effect, probably unintended, of this policy-oriented jurisprudence will be an unconstitutional shift of power from the legislature and the executive to the courts. Democracy, as we know it, will be sacrificed on the altar of judicial policy-making.

Nor is it a defense to emphasize as you do that many legislators today sometimes abdicate their legislative duty by enacting vague statutes whose meaning is left to be determined by the courts. This lamentable legislative dereliction cannot be transformed into a basis for an expanded jurisdiction for the courts. A legislative vice does not translate into a judicial duty. The constitutionally mandated balance of powers cannot be amended by such legislative default and judicial acquiescence or even eagerness to remedy this default. Let me be perfectly clear here: I am no political Scrooge. I agree that migrant farmworkers suffer a "plight" that stirs my political and compassionate conscience and, in my private persona as a citizen, I support migrant-aid legislation and executive action to aid them as well as private-sector charities that help them. In my persona as judge, however, I have a question for Judge Freedom and her judicial fellow travelers: If changing "political and social ideologies" and "physical and social facts" such as those emerging in "a modern industrialized and urbanized society" as well as "time-marches-on" concepts of "stewardship" in property drive your judicial reasoning, **how do you distinguish in principle between judicial reasoning and decision-making and political reasoning and decision-making by the legislature and the executive?**

I conclude my rebuttal with another question for Judge Freedom and her cohorts: Should *Shack* now be overruled by the New Jersey Supreme Court since the left-leaning "social and political" ideologies of the

1960's that underpin *Shack* are now replaced by the right-leaning "social and political ideologies" of the 1980's? For my part, these sophistic arguments by Judge Freedom lead me to affirm even more strongly the classic principled distinction between law and political ideology, and between law and morality.

Judge Pragmatic

Though my esteem for Judges Vigorous and Freedom is unbounded, respect for the truth of who we are and what we are about as judges leads me to a deep sense of regret and sadness. How can such distinguished judges prattle on with such jurisprudential theologies. Their arguments are wondrous examples of the power of self-delusion to blind us to the facts of what we actually do as judges.

Judge Vigorous, who believes that law and democratic politics are as separate as heaven and hell, used to dwell in Dante's inferno herself. A long-time activist in unsavory clubhouse politics, she obtained her judicial appointments not from God or from the legal fairy but from the mayor and later the governor. Perhaps her well-cultivated distrust for democratic politics, and her need as a judge to distance herself from it, flows from the fact that most of the political support for her judicial appointments came from former associates who now confer daily in the exercise yard of state prison.

The triumphant fallacy

Though Judge Vigorous' analysis abounds with fallacies, perhaps the triumphant fallacy is that the principle of separation of powers among the legislative, executive and judiciary, requires a completely separate jurisprudential justification and a unique judicial methodology. That is false. We are all— whether legislators, mayors, governors or judges—participants engaged in a common enterprise: the challenging art and craft of democratic government in response to the needs of our people. We share core democratic values which have emerged from our historical experience and which have enabled an astonishingly diverse people to prosper. We must all serve these values in our concrete tasks. We must never forget that we judges too are either elected by the people or appointed by elected mayors, governors and the president. We are not above the democratic fray.

In a pathetic game, many judges pretend we are distinguished from our legislative and executive colleagues because our exercise of discretion is fenced in by legal rules. Unlike legislators and governors, we apply the so-called "legal model," whereby we apply "the objective propositional meaning of the statutory and case rules" (Judge Vigorous). While I realize that old fictions die slowly, I had thought that the image of the judge as simply an impartial disciple of the doctrine of **stare decisis**, a devotee of fact-finding and rule-applying, a kind of "slot-machine automaton" who feeds on facts and spews out rules and decisions, had faded in deference to widespread recognition, in Professor Delaney's words, that "trial and appellate judges exercise substantial and inescapable discretion in applying and interpreting rules from cases and statutes" (*supra*, p. 76).

Discretion is decisive

Judges must exercise such discretion, *inter alia,* "in deciding whether or not the facts and issues presented in a new case are similar to the facts and issues in a prior case cited as a precedent" (*supra* pp. 75-76); "in deciding exactly how to apply a judge-made rule contained in the holding of the prior case to the new case," either extending or limiting the rule by selecting either a broad or narrow view of the old holding (*supra*, p. 75); in deciding "which of two or more clearly or arguably applicable precedents presented by opposing lawyers should be applied in a new case" (75); in deciding which meaning included in an open-textured statutory or case word is applicable in a particular case (76); and in determining, even with more concrete statutory and case words, the precise scope of coverage of such words, keeping in mind that legal rules are embodied in words and "words are intrinsically a storehouse of ambiguity" (p. 76).

I could continue this litany of everyday occasions that require the exercise of "substantial and inescapable discretion" by trial and appellate judges (see, e.g., p. 75), but I find it more illuminating to concentrate on the amazing fact that Judge Vigorous and her judicial fellow-travelers prefer to slight, or even to omit altogether, the reality that the exercise of judicial discretion is the true ground for choosing one rule rather than another, one meaning over another in applying open-ended principles, etc. I have long suspected that the reason for this glaring oversight is that acknowledgment of the centrality of discretion in decision-making explodes the false image of the judge as a high priest or as an objective arbiter who simply finds facts and applies neutral rules and principles to the facts to resolve controversies, impliedly enlisting the aura of legitimacy bestowed both by religion and science. Such evasion and posturing must be exposed.

To anticipate a rebuttal that legal principle can provide the ground for the inevitable choices that judges must make, the manifest response is—Which principle is chosen to be the guide and why? An exercise of discretion, wise or otherwise, usually for practically oriented ends, also controls the selection of one principle rather than another. And finally, since I notice Judge Freedom chuckling, I have a question for the judge—What is the ground for your selection of one policy over another as the basis for your policy-oriented decision making? Isn't it equally clear again that the answer is an exercise, hopefully wise, of judicial discretion?

A veil of self-deception

Once we penetrate the dense veil of self-deception, we can see that the notion that our fact-finding and rule-applying is uniquely fenced in by the "legal model," thereby distinguishing ourselves from legislators and executors, is false, a product of the inherently impoverished quest for a separate justification for judicial decision making.

Comparably false is the occasional effort to distinguish what we do by rooting it in matters of principle while legislators and executives soil their hands in the dirty pits of utility and pragmatism. Only those who have never heard social security defended as a principled right of old people, or capital punishment defended or criticized on the principle of just deserts, could urge such a patently self-serving argument.

Differences

Naturally, there are important differences in detail between and among the legislative process, the executive process and the judicial process, as we all cooperate in the common enterprise of democratic government. But Judge Vigorous and even Judge Freedom make too much of these differences, as if we existed in separate Platonic essences in Plato's Heaven of Ideas. In the real booming, bustling world of legal experience, it is a commonplace observation that the federal executive has thousands of administrative-law judges performing the judicial role and some states have hundreds of such judges; that Congress mandates that the General Accounting Office, a vast administrative agency, report to it and not to the executive; that judges are drawn into supervising administration in bankruptcy, school desegregation, prisoner-rights and other cases, either directly or through court-appointed masters. Only through the most formal or simplistic of high-school-civics lens can we blink at these shared functions in the common enterprise of government.

Cooperation for the common good

On the level of problem-solving, cooperation among the various governmental agencies to maximize the common good must be the guiding philosophy. To illustrate, the Congress enacts and changes the social security law but it is dependent on a faithful implementation of that law by the executive, and it also depends on a wise adjudication of individual claims, both by the administrative-law judges who work for the Social Security Administration and by the federal district court judges who hear appeals from the decisions of the administrative-law judges. In addressing the problem of crime, a state legislature heightens penalties for serious offenses and authorizes drug-prevention programs, which are implemented by judges and by state administrative agencies. As these examples demonstrate, problem-solving by government is common to all three branches of government and only the function of these branches in contributing to the solution differs.

For this cooperation to be truly effective in securing the common good of our people, **a wise exercise of discretion is the *sine qua non*.** The most democratic legislature, executive and judiciary will all flounder without a common-sense approach to these problems, a willingness to share, cooperate and compromise for the sake of the public good. Thus, judges, just as legislators and administrators, must use maximum flexibility to attain the common interest, not just vindicate parochial professional interests, as they decide legal controversies. Precedent and statute are not forgotten, but their application must serve practical ends. They are means, not ends in themselves. When precedents and statutes conflict or the interests of the judiciary, the executive and the legislator clash, we engage in a **practical balancing of the various interests at stake** in order to resolve the controversy. Thus, it is not so much the abstract law-in the-books that is decisive but, rather, the flexible use of this law-in-the-books to attain desirable social ends in law-in-action that is our true raison d'être.

Unlike both Judges Vigorous and Freedom, the law is not a metaphysic or a sort of legal theology. Our jurisprudence must be pragmatic and utilitarian, akin to the temper and experience of the American people. Our animating legal spirit must match the spirit and temper of our people that have made American great. **The real criteria for a judge in exercising discretion in deciding issues by applying doctrine are: What works? What is useful?**

Application to the cases

Applying my practical, result-oriented jurisprudence to Professor Delaney's cases, both *Sauer* (*supra*, pp. 59-60) and *Greaves* (*supra*, pp. 63-64) illustrate that discretion is decisive in legal reasoning and decision making. A well-established but vague legal standard—which dangers ought to have been foreseen in the exercise of reasonable care (*supra*, p. 60)—is applied to two closely related fact situations (*supra*, pp. 59-60 and pp.63-64). In fact, though not in formal legal metaphysics, a practical judgment is made under the guise of applying the vague standard of reasonable care, a practical judgment that actually inspires many decisions, though this fact is shrouded in obscuring and mystifying legal mumbo-jumbo.

To illustrate more specifically, the majority of the judges in *Greaves* disagreed with the minority who feared that a finding of liability would "would so sterilize camp activity for boys as to render it sedentary" (p. 64). Given their exercise of discretion as to which policy was at stake, it is axiomatic that the minority then applied the negligence standard to find no liability. But given a rejection of this minority selection of decisive policy, it is equally axiomatic that the majority applied the negligence rule to find liability. On both sides, the unmistakable ground of decision-making is the contrasting exercise of discretion for or against the cited policy. The judges, of course, prefer to shroud this reality in their majority and minority opinions, but that is an old, and expected, pretense.

The holdings and judgments in *Woods* and *Shack* also illustrate practical decision-making, a balancing of conflicting interests and an arguably wise exercise of discretion in selecting a particular policy as decisive, but the justifying legal mumbo-jumbo soars to byzantine levels.

[Judge Vigorous' face reddens while Judge Freedom fumes and Judge Just appears depressed, all in reaction to Judge Pragmatic's presentation; then Judges Vigorous and Freedom demand and receive a two minute rebuttal.]

Judges Vigorous' and Freedom's Rebuttal

We two judges (Vigorous and Freedom) have our differences but we can happily join together to oppose this predatory crackpot realism that threatens the presuppositions of almost a thousand years of common-law judicial decision-making.

One of the foundational mistakes inherent in Judge Pragmatic's analysis is that he prostitutes the historic role of a judge in deciding the specific legal controversy presented by the particular litigants into a sculptor's clay with which to mold policy for the "public good." The interests of the parties in technical and fair adjudication of their dispute is examined from the standpoint of which reasoning and result will best promote the "public interest." This broad pragmatic (what works) and utilitarian (what is useful) framework for judicial decision making overlooks the duty of judges to respect private rights and interests—to decide only the specific controversy presented to them for decision by the parties.

Democratic theory and practice promotes both individual and minority rights and interests as well as promoting the general interest. Even valid pragmatic and utilitarian claims about the interest of a great majority of our citizens should not defeat the claim of a basic right asserted by a single individual. Judges have a traditional responsibility to protect individual and minority rights and interests against the will of transient majorities. The common interest at stake in each case is embodied in the parties' right to judicial adjudication of their controversy rather than translating their specific conflict into a license to roam broadly in a Quixotic quest for promotion of the public good by manipulation of the specific controversy presented by the parties.

Judge Pragmatic therefore forsakes almost a thousand years of experience, theory building and craft in judicial decision-making of specific controversies in favor of this Quixotic search for the public interest, for which judges are equipped by no special experience, theory or technique. The problems are obvious: whose version of the public interest in a diverse society should the judge adopt; which pragmatic and utilitarian claims of effectiveness and benefit should be preferred by the judge? Shouldn't the judge employ platoons of social philosophers, sociologists and researchers to address these questions in a serious way? And if such platoons of specialists were put to work, should not their reports be subject to public hearings? And if all this be done, what is left for the people's elected representatives to do in Congress and state legislatures? Judges should be content to contribute to the public weal by concentrating on their judicial role in settling specific controversies, to which task they bring to bear much experience, some theory, and considerable craft.

Judge Just

In the tradition of Socrates, Aristotle, Thomas Aquinas, and many of the great common-law judges, I argue that both the validity and vitality of law springs from its conformity to core principles of our moral heritage. The law we fashion specifies a partial answer to that ancient query for any people: What is important? How should we live? The inescapable metaphysical heart of those questions and answers is clear if we realize that such questions and answers presuppose related questions and answers: What is the purpose of life, and how should we live in accordance with our deeply held metaphysical beliefs? Though many without a classical education but with a modern temper of thought will deny it, these questions, and their disparate answers, are not simply for metaphysicians. They are also, in a more concrete sense, for legislators, governors, mayors, judges and lawyers, for all those who engage in the classic art and craft of government.

Moral beings—moral conceptions

The reason is that in essence we are moral beings seeking in our desperate contradiction-filled lives to personify a personal moral vision of what it means to be human. Since we cannot live and personify any such vision without interaction with others, the social, political and legal enterprise is inevitably rooted in explicit and implicit metaphysical presuppositions. Thus, for example, our Declaration of Independence proudly proclaims:

We hold these truths to be self-evident, that all men are created equal, that they are endowed by their Creator with certain unalienable rights, that among these are Life, Liberty and the Pursuit of Happiness.

Isn't it clear beyond quibble that criminal law, civil and criminal procedure, torts, contracts, will, trusts and, indeed, each subject, is permeated with broad and specific moral conceptions. All of these subjects specify partial moral answers to the ancient questions: How shall we live? What is most important? To ignore these moral underpinnings is to ignore what drives us, what is most important about our humanity...it is to engage in massive self-deception.

The historic challenge for judges, as for legislators and executives, and for all those inspired by the seminal philosophers and jurisprudential thinkers within our Western Tradition, is to add twentieth-century glosses to our impressive philosophical, political and legal heritage, to decide the new cases and their particular controversies with the luminous light cast by that Western Heritage. I hasten to add quickly that we judges can add important new insights to this tradition—we are inspired by our heritage, not prisoners of it.

[Judge Pragmatic yawns and asks—"With all respect, we have heard this many times before. Please turn to Professor Delaney's cases"].

Judge Just continues

Gladly, though I do so with necessary comment on what has been said here today by my distinguished brethren. Judge Vigorous' perspective on law is like discussing Michaelangelo solely by reference to his paints and brushes, Einstein by his calculations, or Gandhi by his lawyerly skill. What is glaringly omitted in such reductive distortions is Michaelangelo's artistic vision, Einstein's scientific vision, and Gandhi's moral vision and leadership.

So too, Judge Vigorous would strip the law of its distinctly human essence, its moral and metaphysical dimensions, reducing it to a circumscribed ambit of authorizing rules, methods and techniques. The utter moral bankruptcy of this example of a modern technocratic refuge from the primordial questions of life is that legal positivism would validate with the proud banner of law even Hitlerite and Stalinist statutes and resulting massacres and other persecutions. At most, these would be moral, not legal, abominations. Though now waning in influence, this triumph of technocratic reasoning is only understandable as a corollary of our secular, technocratic era and its transient, albeit cannibalistic, passions.

A rootless, atomistic activism

Both Judges Freedom and Pragmatic suffer from a shared judicial malady which is also typical of our age: a rootless atomistic activism, devoid of a driving, justifying jurisprudence. As *Shack* illustrates, we are afflicted with a typical American eclecticism, a Judicial porridge made of bits of empiricism, sociology, history, politics, and congressional intent, all served up under the obscuring and incoherent rubric of "policy considerations." Let me be absolutely clear: Judicial activism, whether left-leaning as in *Shack* or right-leaning as in *Woods*, may be justified, but it must be morally principled, not opportunistic, holistic, not atomistic.

As for Judge Pragmatic's puerile pragmatism and utilitarianism as guiding lights for judicial decision-making, my first reaction was that he was engaged in an artful parody that could be performed as television entertainment, perhaps on "Saturday Night Live." While its exposition by Judge Pragmatic is surely its best refutation, suffice it for me to say that neither pragmatism nor utilitarianism can supply coherent ends (nor positivism or policy). An adequate jurisprudence linked to general philosophy and ethics can. As for balancing conflicting interests, how on earth is that to be rationally accomplished without a coherent jurisprudence to provide criteria for such balancing? Balancing without a coherent framework for balancing is like an acrobat traversing a high wire—without the wire.

A claim of justice

While the quality of jurisprudential reasoning in all of Professor Delaney's cases is hardly impressive, at least Judge Desmond in *Woods* (*supra*, pp. 79-84) formulates and analyzes the controversy by explicitly acknowledging a claim of justice as the true ground of the decision, what many modern judges, in a tour de force of self-deception, prefer to obscure and mystify as simply "logic," "analysis" or "facts". Their provincial twentieth century presuppositions, whether ontological, epistemological or moral, are all magically transformed into statements of logic, analysis or fact, as if these judges were simply neutral, white-coated laboratory scientists yearning to uncover the truths of nature.

While *Woods* is also replete with technical reasoning, (*supra*, pp. 79-84), that technical reasoning illustrates the proper role for craft—as the servant of moral principle. My legal conscience compels me, however, to note that Judge Desmond's opinion is devoid of any grounding of his claim of justice in moral philosophy, a typically superficial American approach, as if the mere claim in itself is sufficient since no judge on the court cared to dispute it. Imagine what Socrates would do with this form of modernist reasoning. ["Enough," Judge Pragmatic shouts as he stands up looking apoplectic and starts towards Judge Just. Judges Vigorous and Freedom, though also provoked, intervene and coax Pragmatic to sit down. All three judges demand rebuttal time].

Rebuttal by Judges Vigorous Freedom and Pragmatic

Though we have our profound differences, we can all agree that Judge Just's natural-law twaddle is of no help whatever in the real world of judicial decision-making. To illustrate, how does metaphysics aid Justice Oliver W. Holmes in *McBoyle* to determine whether an airplane is a "vehicle" or aid the Supreme Court of Iowa to determine if the facts in *Port Huron* spell out a unilateral offer and acceptance (Judge Vigorous); how does metaphysics aid the New York appellate judges in *Sauer* and *Greaves* in determining if the camp counselors' duty of reasonable care imposed a duty to foresee the dangers that materialized (Judge Pragmatic); and how does metaphysics aid the New Jersey Supreme Court in *Shack* in resolving the conflict in rights between the farmowner and the migrant farmworkers (Judge Freedom)?

Even in *Woods* where there is a claim of justice, there is absolutely no specification of metaphysics as its root, an omission pedantically criticized by Judge Just. The claim of justice in *Woods* is a concrete, lawyerly claim that reflects a practical choice among available options, a prudential, not a metaphysical, judgment, illustrating that justice is no monopoly of Judge Just and his judicial fellow-travelers. The underlying fallacy is Just's presupposition that judges cannot agree upon and apply a moral/legal claim such as justice without also agreeing upon the metaphysical nature and ground of the claim. The error of this presupposition is revealed not simply by analysis: It is also refuted by thousands of cases in which a standard of justice has been applied to resolve specific controversies without any metaphysical posturing.

As his comments demonstrate, Judge Just excels at irrelevant theorizing as well as invective, but the last concern of busy real-life judges in a secular, pluralistic society should be metaphysical questing for "the origin and purpose of life." Perhaps Judge Just's temperament would flower if he taught jurisprudence or general philosophy at a university, perhaps ideally in Europe.

[Suddenly, the door to the room opens and Judge Crit walks in, complaining that "Professor Delaney's invitation to me was apparently misdirected." The other judges look embarrassed and someone loudly alludes to "administrative deficiencies" in the court.]

Judge Crit

While I have missed your presentations today, I have suffered through them often enough in the past so that I am not disadvantaged.

Law in every society is primarily a weapon of the powerful to legitimate and entrench their domination over oppositionists and the powerless. There is therefore **no principled distinction between law and politics**. Hence, the politics of domination and oppression necessarily involves an implementing law of domination and oppression. In Russia, Czarist politics and law oppressed the serfs and battalions of reformers, including the Bolshevik dissidents. When Lenin seized power, Leninist law, and soon Stalinist law, served to legitimate the slaughter of millions and the destruction of all organized, even all public, opposition. Until recently and even after decades of growing legal sophistication, political and legal oppression of religious, ethnic and civil libertarian dissidents was in accord with the norms of socialist jurisprudence and legality. For example, penal statutes prohibited oral or written "slander" of the socialist political, economic or social system with state procurators (prosecutors) and judges manipulating the meaning of "slander" to meet current political exigencies.

Our own history too bursts with proof. The American revolutionaries ("the slaveherders who wanted freedom") created a federal Constitution with a so-called "Charter of Liberties" for themselves while simultaneously cloaking slavery for blacks with a constitutional framework. Slaves were not participants in this social contract. Rather, they were victims of it. Reeking with hypocrisy, these slaveherders for freedom, whose concept of freedom included the right to enslave blacks, used the masking word of servitude to hide their legitimation of slavery and even legitimized the monstrous slave trade until 1808. The three-fifths compromise empowered the slaveholders to count the slaves in calculating representation in the federal House of Representatives, while denying slaves all the human rights they themselves cherished and protested about. Lest any slave seek emancipation by fleeing, as many did, the Constitution explicitly authorized the Congress and the states to enact fugitive slave acts—and many did so. With the constitutional legitimation of slavery, slave law embedded slavery not only as an economic, political and social reality but also as an entrenched American legal reality with elaborate black codes and a matching array of common-law case law. Slaves were contractually sold like sugar, feed or pigs. Even after emancipation, new black codes in many states aided in transforming the old slavery into the new black serfdom. Later, Jim Crow laws capped this use of law to dominate and manipulate the black minority. Similarly too, Native Americans were excluded from the constitutional/legal compact. They too were victims of it by exclusion, by constitutionally authorized treaties laden with bad-faith, by state removal acts forcing them to leave their ancestral lands for far-away reservations, and by eventual genocide in many cases. Our laws also played key roles in the oppression of workers (organizing was a "conspiracy" and injunctions proliferated); and in the subordination of women. "We the people" did not include Blacks, Native Americans or women, much more than a majority of the people.

[At this point, Judge Just interrupts Judge Crit: "On behalf of the other judges, we apologize for the regrettable fact that our scheduled time has expired. Perhaps you will be able to continue your diatribe on another occasion." Professor Delaney interjects that the scheduled time could be extended, especially in light of the "administrative deficiencies" within the court that resulted in Judge Crit's invitation being "misplaced" and his resulting late arrival. After a quick murmuring-type conference with the other judges, Judge Just expresses their appreciation to Professor Delaney for his kind suggestion but indicates firmly that they "decline to extend the scheduled time," and the meeting is quickly adjourned by Judge Just leading the hasty exit of the other judges.]

Comments by Professor Delaney

The manufacture of legal meaning

These introductory presentations of contrasting jurisprudential perspectives illustrate that legal meaning is not captured simply in the objective statutes and cases, the court houses, or even the often ritual behavior of lawyers, judges, clerks, clients and witnesses. Nor is legal meaning simply subjective, a subjective creation of each judge. Rather, legal meaning, as all meaning, is manufactured in an unending inter-subjective interaction of the judges, lawyers, litigants, etc. with the statutes, cases, and other materials. In the manufacturing of multiple legal meanings, the following insights have proved useful to me.

A bit of semiology

In the eloquent words of Paul Ricoeur:

"...human action is an open work, the meaning of which is 'in suspense.' It is because it 'opens up' new references and receives fresh relevance from them, that human deeds are also waiting for fresh interpretations which decide their meaning. All significant events and deeds are, in this way, opened to this kind of practical interpretation through present praxis",

Hermeneutics and the Human Sciences 208 (1981)

Do you see-how such open-ended statutory and case principles, such as "equitable," "just," "fair," "reasonable," and "proper," are partly determined by prior meanings embodied in a stream of cases, but also "in suspense," inviting the "fresh interpretations which decide their [unfolding] meaning." The moral content of these general principles is therefore partly fixed in the sense of the stream of past cases and partly indeterminate and thus open in that the stream from the past flows into the unfolding present. As new frameworks of meaning crystallize from evolving political, economic, cultural and technical evolution, the moral meaning of equitable, fair, just, etc., changes in the culture, and these evolving moral meanings infiltrate into the fresh interpretations urged and imposed by lawyers arguing and judges deciding specific controversies that exemplify the new meanings. As a vivid example, consider the fresh meanings of the legal words, "parent" and "child," and the usual standard for determining custody cases of the "best interests of the child," in light of in vitro conception and emerging categories of genetic parent (the woman whose egg is fertilized or the man whose sperm is utilized); the uterine parent (the woman who gestates a fertilized egg of another woman); the natural parent in a traditional sense; the psychological parent (foster parent); etc. Consider the implications of the newly created categories in determining who is a parent, child, sibling, grandparent, uncle and aunt for purposes of intestacy, wills, trusts and estates. These emerging and complexifying meanings profoundly alter our ideas of human identity and will reverberate throughout the law. But some of these distinctions would have been characterized as science fiction ten or fifteen years ago. While the interpretation in *Shack* of the old state trespass statute in light of congressional intent and purpose in the new federal anti-poverty statutes is a dramatic example of "human action" as an "open work," inviting "fresh interpretations" by the courts, routine cases, including *Sauer* and *Greaves* (*supra*, pp. 57-63), also illustrate the identical potential. The reason that these prosaic cases illustrate this potential is that the standard at stake—the duty of the camp supervisors to "guard against dangers which ought to have been foreseen in the exercise of reasonable care"—is a virtual invitation in its breadth and open-endedness—to "fresh interpretations" in light of new fact patterns and evolving conceptions of reasonableness that reflect unfolding dangers, fears and feminist values. Consider, for example, the meaning of "reasonable" in light of uncovering the horrific dangers of asbestos, DES, proliferating toxic torts, and the risks of nuclear power, especially measured against the rising consciousness of rights.

Institutional constraints on the judge as Lone Ranger

Lest you jump from the conclusion that law is simply a narrow technical reality to the conclusion that a judge is simply a judicial Lone Ranger who shoots from the hip, let me assure you that jurisprudential choices are not simply indeterminate, nor simply a matter of a judicial menu for individual selection. They are significantly bridled by institutional restraints imposed by shared understandings, the judge's role in the judicial system, the fashion of a particular judicial era, and by all manner of other related reasons.

Common shared understandings in the legal culture

First, at a minimum, the subject-matter at issue often comes laden with an entrenched historical repertoire of underlying jurisprudential choices, which comprise a complex of common understandings shared among judges who decide such cases, an expression of the legal culture, a sub culture in American society. Judges are socialized into this legal culture first as lawyers, usually for many years, and later as new judges. They typically come to personify a set of intellectual and moral traditions, of common expectations, of a repertoire of acceptable values and modes of thinking. To illustrate, strict construction of criminal statutes to vindicate the principles of legality, due-process fairness and separation of powers is a jurisprudential choice embedded in countless statutes, cases and in judicial consciousness. Thus, the decision of a trial or appellate judge who departed from this tradition would likely receive special scrutiny to determine if the factual or legal exigencies posed by the particular case warranted the departure. Even in criminal law, however, there are multiple exceptions to this embedded jurisprudential choice. These include, for example, the Racketeer Influenced Corrupt Organization Act (RICO) statute that mandates flexible and broad construction, the state statutory clones of RICO, the federal mail-fraud statute, and key statutory provisions in military law. In sharp contrast, judicial decision-making of an equitable issue— e.g., equitable-distribution of martial property in a divorce action or determining custody of a child by the standard of "the best interest of the child"—invites, even compels, the application of broad spectrum judicial reasoning, another jurisprudential choice equally embedded in countless cases and in the judicial consciousness. Hence, the decision of any judge who conspicuously departed from this tradition in deciding such cases would also likely receive special scrutiny to assess whether the factual or legal exigencies posed by the particular case warranted the departure. Thus, the historically given repertoire of choice(s) creates expectations that particular types of legal reasoning will be applied. Such expectations, however, are not cast iron shackles.

Role in the judicial system

Second, jurisprudential choice by judges is also somewhat bridled by the **level of court** in which the judge performs. A trial judge must respect the spectrum of such choices embedded not only in the state's statutes but also in the case law embedded in the decisions of that state's appellate courts, especially the highest court. Trial judges generally choose within these spectrums. A trial-court choice of legal reasoning beyond the relevant spectrum of choices may invite special appellate scrutiny if there is an appeal. While appellate judges also reason within the spectrum of choices, their freedom to limit, extend, revise and add to the existing choices is empowered by the fact that the existing authoritative cases flowed in the past from the same appellate courts. The doctrine of *stare decisis* requires respect for existing authority by the present appellate judges, but not a slavish obedience where change is mandated by new facts, needs and values (e.g., *Woods*, pp. 79-84) This latter truth has special force for the judges who comprise the highest court in each state.

Current traditions of the court

Third, Professor Karl N. Llewellyn stressed the **"current tradition of the court"** as influential in the "craft of judging." He distinguishes the "Grand Style" prevalent in "1820-1850" during which "our courts felt in general a freedom and duty" in which "Precedent" guided but "Principle" controlled; and "nothing was good" "Principle" "which did not look like wisdom in result for the welfare of all-of-us." Llewellyn then contrasts this "Grand Style" with the "Formal Style" of the late nineteenth and early twentieth centuries during which our courts felt in general a prime duty to order within the law and a duty to resist any "outside" influence. "Precedent" was to control, not merely guide; tested by whether it made for order in the law, not by whether it made 'wisdom-in-result'. 'Legal' principle could not be subjected to 'political' tests…." Karl N. Llewellyn, "Remarks On The Theory Of Appellate Decisions And The Rules Or Canons About How Statutes Are To Be Construed," 3 *Vanderbilt L.R.*, pp. 395-396 (1950).

Writing in 1950, Llewellyn notes that since 1920 the Formal Style has slowly waned while the Grand Style has revived. For any specific court, he suggests a verification procedure—"the latest volume of reports, read in sequence from page 1 through to the end: the current mine-run of the work" (*Id.*)

Law as fact versus law as hope

Fourth, in addition to the current tradition of the court, Llewellyn also stressed the **"current temper of the court,"** the **"court's tradition as modified by its personnel"** (*Id.*). He stressed what all practicing lawyers know:

> the constellation of the personnel on a particular bench at a particular time plays its important part in urging the court toward a more literal or a more creative selection among the available accepted and correct 'ways' of handling precedent (Id. at 397).

Selznick reflects this reality in a larger context of law and legal culture:

"In the discussion of law, there is an ever-renewed conflict between those who see it as a functional necessity and others who invest it with hope and promise. The former accept law as a given, as fact, at best as an instrument of practical problem solving. For the legal idealist, on the other hand, law connotes a larger moral achievement "

Selznick, Law Society and Moral Evolution, in Readings In Jurisprudence and Legal Philosophy 930 (Schuman ed. 1979).

This contrasting judicial proclivity reflects two contrasting personal temperaments, politics and even mythologies: first, the judge "who loves order, who finds risk uncomfortable" who interprets "responsibility" as "caution" and who views "reorientation of the law in our polity as essentially committed to the legislature." The contrasting judicial temperament, politics and mythology, though shadings are more common than pure types, is the person "who loves creativeness, who can ... combine risk-taking with responsibility, who sees and feels institutions as things built and to be built to serve functions, and who sees ... law as a tool to be eternally reoriented to justice and to general welfare" (*Llewellyn* at 397). This latter judge almost instinctively seizes each opportunity to make the law a little better, more logical and just, more responsive to current problems and values.

Lastly, Llewellyn, stressed **"the sense of the situation as seen by the court,"** which can lead a court strongly influenced by the first more literal temperament to move into "tremendous creative expansion of precedent" while a court strongly influenced by the second temperament "will happily and literally apply a formula ... if a formula makes sense and yields justice in the situation and the case" (*Id*. at 397).

Conclusion

It is a mistake to view these contrasting traditions, judicial temperaments, politics, mythologies and senses of the situation, as undermining the law. Such a view presupposes what does not exist: a single, true and monolithic perspective on the meaning and role of law in our society. Rather, these polarities are central to the law viewed as a human enterprise and to the jurisprudential choices inherent in it. Those who would openly or covertly reduce law to a single jurisprudential perspective are evading this complexity and the inescapable need for choice and for justification of such choice.

Adios.

Appendix A

Abbreviations for Briefing Cases

Below is an alphabetical list of abbreviations for use in briefing cases. Since your briefs are for your benefit, however, use whatever abbreviations help you. These abbreviations can give you ideas for other abbreviations.

A	agent	ct. app.	court of appeals (state)
A.B.A.J.	American Bar Association Journal	cir. ct. app.	circuit court of appeals (state)
adm'r	administrator	city ct.	city court
aff'd	affirmed	civ. app.	civil appeals
A.L.I.	American Law Institute	civil pro.	civil procedure
A.L.J.	American Law Judge	C.J.	Corpus Juris
A.L.R.	American Law Reports	C.J.S.	Corpus Juris Segundum
answ.	answer	c/l or c.l.	common law
app., apps.	appendix(ices)	C.M.A.	Court of Military Appeals
app. div.	appellate division	C.M.R.	Court of Military Review
art., arts.	article(s)		
assoc.	associate	compl.	complaint
atty.	attorney	comm.	committee
B	buyer or beneficiary	Cong.	Congress
bfp	bona fide purchaser	cons.	constitutional
b/k	breach of contract	cr.	creditor
bk., bks.	book(s)	crim. app.	criminal appeals
BNA	Bureau of National Affairs	crim. l.	criminal law
		D	defendant
brd	beyond a reasonable doubt	dam.	damages
c/a	cause-of-action	deb.	debtor
CCH	Commerce Clearing House	def.	defense
		dir.ver.	directed verdict
cert.	certiorari	dist.	district
ch., chs.	chapter(s)	ev.	evidence
cir. ct.	circuit court of appeals (federal)	em.	employer

ee.	employee	P.	Property (course)
edit.	edition	prop.	property
F.2d	Federal 2nd	pub.	public
fam. ct.	Family Court	reas. man	reasonable man
f/D	for defendant	rev'd	reversed
f.m.	felony murder	S	Seller
f/P	for plaintiff	s/p	specific performance
F.R.D.	Federal Rule Decision	sub. l.	substantive law
Ga.L.R.	Georgia Law Review	sup. ct.	superior court
H	Husband	sup. jud. ct.	supreme judicial court
H.R.	House Report	sur. ct.	surrogate's court
J.	judge, justice	Supp.	Supplement
J J.	judges, justices	T	torts
judg.	judgment	t	trustee or tenant
juris.	jurisdiction	uncon.	unconstitutional
K	contract	U.S.C.	United States Code
L	Landlord	U.S.C.A.	United States Code Annotated
liab.	liability	U.S.D.Ct.	United States District Court
litig.	litigation		
mag.	magistrate	U.S.L.W.	United States Law Week
mot.	motion		
Nat. L.J.	National Law Journal	U.S.Sup.Ct.	United States Supreme Court
neg.	negligence		
N.L.R.B.	National Labor Relations Board	v.	versus
		ver.	verdict
no., nos.	number(s)	W	wife
O	offer	w/i	within
Ord.	order	w/o	without
P	plaintiff		
p., pp.	page(s)		
p/f	prima facie		
pld'g.	pleading		
proc. l.	procedural law		

Appendix B

Another Book and Audiotapes by Professor John Delaney

BOOK:

How To Do Your Best on Law School Exams, 1982, 1988, pp. 235, $19.95, available in most law bookstores. This much-used book, borne of many years of law school teaching, offers a systematic approach to learning law, studying for exams, issue identifying, doing course outlines, avoiding blunders, and outlining and answering law school problems. It includes actual exam problems with illustrative "A" and poor answers and comments explaining why answers are excellent or poor. This book is revised and is in a ninth printing.

AUDIOTAPES:

The Fundamentals of Taking Law School Exams, approximately 4 hours, $29.95. These audiotapes, intended for first year law students and those experiencing difficulty with exams, present an introduction to the taking of law exams; a specification of the exams skills that you must display; the criteria by which you'll be graded; a series of common exam blunders to be avoided; and a detailing of study recommendations which will help you to prepare for exams. These audiotapes also detail a method for identifying issues on law exams with a step-by-step approach, and a method for organizing and writing lawyerly answers. Lastly, the tapes specify suggestions for outlining your courses, designed to aid you in taking exams.

9 780960 851447